Productive TOILET TIME

Quick Inspirational Stories to Read During Your Morning Poop

By Rosilee Barreto

For my husband and our five kiddos.
I'm inspired by each of you more than you know.

Contents

Acknowledgements

A book is always a collaborative effort, and I am sincerely grateful for all who have helped me on this journey. First, I want to give a huge shout-out to the friends and family members who contributed to this book. Your stories inspired me, and I know they will inspire others. I literally could not have done this book without each of you, and I am forever grateful for your support.

I would like to thank Ellaine Ursuy for being an incredible mentor and guide. Her clear direction was invaluable and made this book come together so much faster than I could have ever dreamed. I will forever be grateful for Ellaine and the rest of the amazing team at Self-Publishing School.

A big thanks goes to Wayne Purdin. If I could name him Editor of the Year, I would! I sincerely appreciate the time he spent not only editing the book, but teaching me how to use and understand the tricks to the computer software as well.

Another big thanks goes to Tonye Victor Bagshaw, who was a fantastic find on Upwork.com. He put up with me during endless revisions to the design of the cover and the formatting of this book for publishing.

Finally, I am very grateful for my husband. He thinks every idea I have is crazy, and still lets me do it anyway. I could not have done this without him, or without our children, who pitched in extra around the house to give me more time to write and collect stories. I am surrounded by amazing people, and I am grateful for their loving influence in my life.

Introduction

———

I started reading self-help books in college. My first self-help book was *The 7 Habits of Highly Effective Teens* by Sean Covey. Even though I was in college, the teenage humor included throughout the book made me laugh and kept me reading to the end. After that, I started reading more and more self-help books and was drawn to the world of successful business entrepreneurs.

Years later, when my husband's older children, all teenagers, moved in with us for a bit, I would constantly try to find a way to get them to read about goal setting, finance, or other useful information that I wish I would have known as a teenager. However, my "teaching moments" as I call them, pretty much fell on deaf ears...until the day I started a different tactic: story reading. If I wanted to teach a story about being kind to others, I would find a short story about kindness. If I wanted to teach them about honesty or dependability, I would find a short story to read that taught each concept.

Suddenly, my kids were listening. Sometimes, they would even ask questions afterward or share ideas about how they could apply the principles taught by the main character. A few times, I've asked them what we should do to solve a problem or how to help someone, and heard responses like, "Hey, remember that one story about service you read to us a while ago? Maybe we could do something like that."

When I realized that the short stories I had been reading were actually being heard and applied, I decided to write down some of my own stories from my life that I could share with the kids. After I had written a few of my own stories, I started asking my friends and family members to share stories of people or events that had inspired them or taught them something.

After I had a collection of a few stories, I had the thought that maybe I could gather a few more and publish the stories into an inspirational book for teenagers or young adults. When I told my teenagers I wanted to write a book with a collection of stories to help teach and inspire, our oldest groaned, rolled his eyes, and said, "Well, it better have a funny title. No one's going to read it if it doesn't."

I laughed when he said that but then realized he was right. I thought about my own first experience with self-help books and how I had only read the book to the end because it was funny. But what was considered a funny title to teenagers or even adults?

Ironically, the answer for me came in the form of a TV commercial. My husband and I were watching an episode of *The Good Doctor* when a commercial came on about knowing the difference between healthy poop and sick poop; seriously, that was the commercial.

But what stuck out to me was a phrase that one of the narrators said. It was something to the effect of, "Everyone is looking at their *phones* for 20 minutes during their morning poop when they *should* be looking at their poop."

Suddenly, it hit me; what if I could capture the attention of a few of those people on their phones for 20 minutes during their morning poop? Maybe they still wouldn't be paying attention to whether they had healthy poop or not, but, at least, they could start the morning with an inspirational story!

From there, I started in earnest to collect stories from friends, family, and mentors. I've learned so much about the power that each of us has within us to help and inspire others to greatness. Many of the people in these stories are just regular people (parents, teachers, coaches, friends) but the impact they had on the lives of others was profound.

Sometimes, it just takes one person or one event to completely transform how we view life and how we view ourselves. It has been that way for thousands of people, including world-renowned self-help entrepreneurs. Sean Covey, the author of the book I first read, was inspired by his father, Stephen Covey. Steve Jobs, the creator of Apple, was inspired by a college professor, a monk named Robert Palladino. Tony Robbins, one of the world's most recognized motivational speakers, was inspired by Jim Rohn, a farm boy from Idaho who became a motivational speaking success. Napoleon Hill, author of *Think and Grow Rich*, was inspired by his stepmother, who believed in him when no one else did.

We all have a story of someone or something that inspired us to do something or create something we never would have done without that support. This book is a tribute to those incredible heroes, the majority of whom are not world-renowned or famous; they're just regular people, doing the best they can and helping someone else be a little better as well.

To those of you who've wanted to read a self-help book but have never quite managed to finish to the end, this book is for you. You'll find little nuggets of wisdom in the stories of others. Maybe not all of the stories will apply to you, but I guarantee that at least one story in this book will inspire you or give you an idea that could help make your life a little better today than it was yesterday

A few of the stories in this book are religious or talk about God. I'm a religious person and so are some of my friends, whose stories are shared in this book. Since religion is somewhat a topic of debate these days, I offer this information simply as a courtesy to those who may not want to read any stories of a religious nature.

Also, for those of you have never been into reading much and are using this book as a starting point, I encourage you to choose the shortest story in this book and start reading there. Then move to the next shortest one. All of the stories in this book can be read in less than 20 minutes, some in 5 minutes or less! So, pick a story and start reading. When you hit that nugget of wisdom you've been searching for, you'll be glad that you did!

How My First Coach Inspired Me to Become a Coach - and I Didn't Even Realize It

By Marisa Raymond

---

 ike many people who grew up before the age of social media, I count my blessings that there aren't photos of me in my preteen and teen years splashed over the internet.

Being a teenager is hard enough.

As a parent of two boys, currently ages 10 and 13, I look back on my childhood with so much more forgiveness and compassion for my parents than I had at the time.

Parenting is one of the hardest jobs you'll ever have. It is a long, winding, rollercoaster with twists and turns, peaks and valleys. Children don't come with blueprints or manuals. As a parent, you often are left feeling out-of-control and unprepared for what each day's ride will look like.

When I look at photos of myself at 13-14, there's a sadness behind my eyes that few people notice, and even fewer people knew about at the time.

On the surface, I'm smiling. And I had a lot to be happy about. I grew up in a middle-class family on New York's Upper West Side. I went to a good school, got good grades, made extra spending money babysitting, and had a smart, funny, diverse group of friends.

We didn't have a pandemic going on like we did in 2020. But the U.S. had just launched Operation Desert Storm and CNN was showing 24/7 coverage of gun battles, burning oil fields, and reading out the names of soldiers killed in action.

And my father was downsized from his job and diagnosed with severe depression.

I lived with a constant cloud over my head. Just waiting for the next shoe to drop, for impending doom.

I felt insecure, struggling with body image issues, trying to fit in and feel like I belonged. I tried to prove my worth by being a "good girl": following the rules, studying hard, taking care of my family, trying to balance the weight of the world on my shoulders.

Then, in the spring of my freshman year of high school, I set a goal to make our school's softball team. And I failed. I was devastated. It was the first time I really felt like I wasn't good enough.

I still remember that feeling in the pit of my stomach when I looked at the roster and didn't see my name on the list.

And I remember the coach of our team, who was also a sports and health education teacher at the school, coming up to me in the hall to tell me that it'd be okay. In a sympathetic voice, he told me that I had great potential, and he was proud of me for showing up. And with a little bit of practice and work, I'd be sure to make the team next year.

The thing about Robert Gaudenzi is that he's genuine. And I was fortunate enough to go to a small school where the teachers knew us by our names. Coach G wasn't being flippant in his comments. He wasn't blowing me off or disregarding my feeling of rejection. In that moment, I felt his encouragement, his belief in me, and I felt that if I believed in myself, and worked a little harder and practiced a little more, I could do it.

At a time when I felt like so much was out of my control, Coach G showed me that there was something I could control: how hard I worked to achieve my goal of making the team.

And, a year later, my name was on that roster.

In so many other areas of my life, I had learned to fear making mistakes, to fear disappointing adults, to fear rejection, to prove my worth through external validation.

Coach G, in that simple belief he had in me and in so many other students like me over the years, planted a seed that has taken decades to sprout into the resilient, grounded, compassionate person that I am today.

Over the course of the next three years, I noticed how Coach G showed genuine interest in each student. He truly seemed to love his job. I remember sitting in a CPR class with him, trying to get the hang of chest compressions and rescue breaths.

He talked to our class with calm and confidence, telling us when the chest of the dummy was high enough that we could stop breathing and start the chest compressions. He encouraged us to connect with the motions, how much air we were breathing, how high the chest was rising.

Now, as a yoga teacher, I realize he was teaching us to be present and mindful in our actions. How to tune out the pending grade and exam result and focus on saving that dummy's life. In fact, as a member of the softball team, he also encouraged us to even use visualization techniques during practice and before games to get into a good head space.

"Center yourself and focus solely on the moment. Concentrate your energy on what you can control. And, win or lose, be genuine and respectful of others."

As a coach, a teacher, a mentor, Coach G always made us feel seen and heard. Like we were a worthy member of the team, whether we were on the starting line or riding the bench. He always made a point to highlight our strengths and point out how we could improve on the weaknesses. His leadership made us feel like a team. And, even as we were doing push-ups and laps, he made sure that we had fun.

I didn't realize how those messages and his role-modeling them in practice would come back to serve me often in the decades since high school, even in tough moments when I faced my own bout of depression, when I moved overseas away from family and friends, and even when I suffered a miscarriage. The seeds he planted grew deep roots and strong branches. Because no matter how dark some moments have been, at some point, I come back to his voice, in the back of my head, telling me I'll get it next time (as "Eye of the Tiger," the soundtrack to our team workouts, plays in the background).

Because really, there's always a next time. There's always an opportunity to learn what you can tweak, how you can adapt, so you can show up differently next time.

It starts with keeping your eye on the ball and focusing your attention on taking it one step at a time. Those seeds can then grow as we become certain, not necessarily of a particular outcome, but of ourselves. Each experience leads us towards more growth, more connections, deeper and stronger values.

And, from that place, we shine our light brightly onto the world, inspire others, and create ripple effects that will change the world.

Marisa Raymond is an American wife, mom, parenting coach, yoga teacher, and genetic counselor living in France. You can connect with her on https:// marisaraymond.com or https://www.facebook. com/mzrcoaching

My Mother's Example

By Cecilia Segedy

Have you ever wondered *Why me? Why is this happening to me. Why do I have to deal with so much pain or unfair things in my life? Is this ever going to end? What am I supposed to learn from this? How is this going to help me in any way?* Well, let me tell you a story about a dear sweet lady who means the world to me.

This sweet lady happens to be my mom. Her name is Jennie and she has dealt with a lot in her life. From her parents getting a divorce to her stepdad saying means things to her that weren't true, she has been belittled in so many ways but has always kept going. Not only did Jennie keep moving forward but she also was able to find the positive in every situation. She was able to turn a bad situation around, find the lesson, and use that lesson to better her life so that she could also better the lives of others around her.

This was true even in the last couple years of her life while she was battling for her life. Jennie was suffering from cancer that had spread clear throughout her body until it finally took her life. She fought a great fight. She was always positive and kept a smile on her face. Jennie was the type of person who would give a stranger the coat off her back if they needed it. She was always looking for ways to serve others and make their lives better.

My dear sweet mom has inspired me and taught me many lessons from the way she lived. The biggest and most important lesson was how to endure to the end. She did this well. Even when it came to raising 12 kids. You may ask yourself how she did it and still have a smile on her face. I ask myself this question multiple times a day as I strive to raise my 6 kids. Jennie would have given her own life for her kids; they were one of her great accomplishments.

Another one of the lessons I've learned from my mom is how to work hard and enjoy working, that when you work hard, you can accomplish great things. She taught me never to give up when things get tough. If you keep going, things will eventually get easier. You'll never know what great things you could have accomplished if you give up before you finish.

I'm so grateful to have known my mom and the inspiration and example she was in my life. Because of my mom, I've grown to love to serve those around me and look for opportunities to serve them. I've also been able to hold my head high and endure my trials as they come. I've been able to find a positive or a blessing from each of my trials.

I wouldn't be the woman I am today without my mom's sweet example in my life. As I strive to lose weight and get healthier to be around longer in life for my kids, I think of my mom's sweet example when the days get tough. That's what keeps me going on my weight loss journey. I would've never made it as far as I have without the sweet inspiration that came from my mom. Some people don't have a mom they can look up to. If you're a parent, I hope you're trying to be one whom your children will be able to look up to. If you're not a parent, you'll still inspire people if you keep going even when you feel like quitting.

So, when things get tough, and you don't know how much longer you can handle it, remember that it's only for a short time and try and find a positive or a blessing that has come from the situation. This trial will pass. Never give up, things always work out in the end.

Unexpected Kindness
By Rosilee Barreto

My senior year in high school, I was taking an AP Calculus class. I've never been great at math, and calculus was extremely difficult for me. Toward the end of the school year, when we were within a month of taking the final exam, I had to go to both early morning and afternoon study groups to understand the concepts that I was consistently getting wrong answers on.

I became obsessed with passing the test. I didn't want all of this hard work and effort I was putting into studying to be in vain.

I had some really great friends my senior year. Most of my friends all wanted to get good grades and go to college, and we really helped each other out. However, because of the stress of this test, I told everyone to leave me alone. Whenever anyone would invite me to hang out or study with them, if it didn't have to do with calculus, I wasn't interested. Pretty soon, most of my friends stopped asking me to hang out and just let me do my own thing.

One friend, however, was constantly telling me I needed to take a break and do something fun, or I was going to burn myself out. I started to really get annoyed by that, and, one day, when she invited me to lunch with her, I snapped. I told her to pretend I didn't exist until this test was over. I felt bad about snapping at her, but I just didn't want any distractions.

A couple hours after school was out, I was sitting at my kitchen table trying to work out some sample problems. Our teacher had given us the answers so that we would know if we got the right answer or not. I couldn't for the life of me figure out the answer to one particular problem. I was almost in tears when I heard a knock on the door.

I grumbled under my breath at the fact that no one else was home and I had to leave what I was doing to answer the door. I also tried to perk up my face, so it wouldn't look like I had been on the brink of crying.

When I opened the door, there was my friend, the one I had yelled at, with a Wendy's chocolate frosty (my favorite ice cream at the time) and a card. Her words kind of rushed out at me before I could even open my mouth. I don't think she even took a breath as she blurted out, "I know you don't want any distractions, so I'm not staying. I just thought you could use some encouragement, and now I'm leaving." Then she handed me the frosty and the card, jumped down the stairs and headed for her car before I could even respond.

I went to the table and opened the card. I don't remember everything that was written, but I remember the last sentence was "You can do it! I believe in you." It was funny, or ironic, not sure...but just at that moment, I realized the mistake I had been making on the problem...and then I started crying.

I had been so mean to that friend, and she had turned around and responded with kindness. And her kindness helped me find a solution to the problem at hand.

I have never forgotten that sincere gesture of kindness from my friend. It was such a simple thing, yet it has stayed with me ever since. We never know what a small act of kindness can do for another human being. I once heard a saying that went, "When in doubt, be kind." I'm so grateful my friend showed kindness toward me, even when she had every reason not to. Her kindness made all the difference.

The Mother I Once Hated

By Adrian Hudson

I don't suppose there is really room to explain it properly. My favorite example in life, at one point, was the person I wanted to mirror less. I wanted to evolve as far away from that influence as possible. I felt she was a burden, a fixed point meant to chain me in place. I wanted an out. And unfortunately, I took it in a direction I now know wasn't the best plan of action. But I suppose this is one of the great parts of being flesh. Human nature means I get to evolve. Just like her. Just like you do.

My Mother's start in life was nothing short of an atypical abuse survival book. She could have written or could write a book similar to *A Child Called It* and probably make decent money. My basic understanding of her childhood is that, to put it bluntly, she was "pimped" out to family and friends for money at an early age. She was coerced into whatever was going on with violence, tricks, etc. I have a bare minimum idea of what happened, but I do know that her father did things like kill her pets in front of her and lock her up in a cage for days to make her pretend she was a pet herself. Ultimately, she and one sibling made it into state's custody where she was fostered by my adoptive grandparents. There, she began to heal, although we know now that some pieces of her will never be whole. Her mind is somewhat permanently like glass that's been hit with a baseball. A perfect web of intertwined trauma and buried memories.

Of course, as childhood abuse and trauma tend to do, this led to some unhealthy patterns. The "Mom" I had as a child and early teen wasn't a mother. She was in and out of treatment facilities. She struggled with self-mutilation, opioid addiction, eating disorders, etc. She wasn't present. And when she was, she didn't behave like an adult. She frequently lost track of time and acted strange. At the time, my parents, in an attempt to spare their children, kept her diagnosis secret from us. There was never truly an explanation as to WHY I mothered my mother. Why my youngest memory of her is busting open the bathroom door to find her slicing her wrists with a can lid and knowing exactly who to call to resolve the issue.

Multiple Personal Disorder. That was what I later learned was her diagnosis, now known as Dissociative Identity Disorder (DID). My childhood trauma compounded on me due to hers. Funny how those circles work isn't it? At age 15, I was finally given some answers. Although, by that point, I wasn't interested in the why or the who. All I knew is this person claiming to be my mother wasn't mine. But let me say, learning about her childhood was the catalyst to what we have now: a relationship, more functional, more mother/

daughter and less dependent/daughter. I began to realize that no one understands trauma and hardship better than my mom. As I was busy making my own mess of life and dealing with my own trauma, she began to be the person I would turn to. At 17, I had my first child, and that event shaped both of us more than I could ever express. As I had started making a catastrophe out of my life, my mother had started to take better steps in hers and make more solid progress. And I'm happy to say that now she's my "person."

My mother as I know her now is the most humble, compassionate, and gentle soul you'll ever meet. She's 3-4-years sober from opioids and addictions. And as I've grown, she has been a steady voice of reason and love. She has met me at my ugliest points and still saw the pieces of me that were begging for help. I'm just Adrian in her eyes. No need to conform or adjust. I'm perfect, capable, strong, and amazing. And if I'm lucky, one day, I'll see myself through her eyes. Through hard work on both sides, we have a different bond now. The biggest part of this is that how I saw her changed, once I took the time and effort to look into her diagnosis and choose to be empowered through educating myself on what she was going through.

I had choices. I could hate her and all the pain I endured. Or I could UNDERSTAND her and embrace the lessons I could take from all of it. In my opinion, whenever embracing a lesson is on the table you should try your best to do that. Educate yourself. Let go of that hot pit in your stomach that churns whenever you think about a person who hurt you. And view the HUMAN BEING across the table with open eyes. The human I see now endured things my own

14

trauma can't compare to, not even close, and she still birthed three intelligent children and came back to try to bat for them in their lives. No one said she needed to do everything perfect. Just that she stood at the plate. She never raised a hand to me, even though that was all she had known as a child. She believed in me when no one else did. She tried to fix her wrongs. She stood up EVERY single time life handed her a blow and kept walking. She held a job for over a decade, even with setbacks that made holding a job seem impossible.

My mother is like a meadow of soft petals and quiet breezes along the alfalfa. She's an example that your roots don't define the fruit you bear, blossoming is a choice, kindness is always an option, and that I can do hard things, even when I feel I can't breathe. Grateful isn't a close enough word to describe how I feel toward her presence. She's so much of me, sown into every part of the fabric that encases my tired soul. And without her as my example of overcoming obstacles, I would fail the test of life miserably. My lens on life has eternally changed because I have her in my heart. That's something I cannot change, nor would I ever want to.

Thank you, Mom. God made you for me.

Educating Yourself Into Opportunities

By Hilary Hinrichs

For myself, I was raised in Iowa and never really felt like I "fit in." I felt like the black sheep of my family. I know I was given many opportunities that were possible in my hometown, and I'm grateful for all of them, yet I knew there was something more I was missing, and it never felt quite like where I wanted to be as I got older.

Growing up in a small town in Iowa in the 90s, leaving the country to travel, let alone even leaving the state, wasn't something people did very often. Even though I'm happy with where I grew up because it led me to be who I am today, I knew there was so much more to learn and experience.

Going to college was really the first glimpse of what it might feel like to leave my small town and experience something new. Little did I know that continuing my education would teach me so much more than just what was in a textbook. This is where I first learned that Christopher Columbus wasn't who we were taught in grade school. This is where I fell in love with philosophy and critical thinking. This is also where I was told that living in the big metropolis of New York City was a possibility. This may sound funny or maybe some can relate to this, but I didn't even know people could live inside New York City before my college professors nonchalantly mentioned there were several students living as well as working there. My jaw dropped to the floor with this knowledge. I'm sure this city didn't appeal to every student in the class, but something told me right away that I must move there.

After learning this, I began to dream even bigger of what my life could look like in one of the biggest cities in the world. Just knowing what was possible gave me the courage to believe.

I then attended a creative writing course for my electives. I wasn't expecting too much from this class, yet I gained more than I ever thought I would. This was the class that truly changed my life because of one professor. He led his class in a very different way that I definitely appreciated. We would debate over topics that were quite controversial, write stories about our lives in a nonjudgmental format, and read books that truly changed my life.

Before this class, I was told most of my life that I wasn't very good at school. I now believe this was mostly due to standardized testing and labeling, but this teacher gave me hope that I was actually capable of so much more. He focused on all students' strengths instead of weaknesses and gave me my first glimpse of what individuality really looked like. He made me

17

believe that it was okay to be different. I leaned into this and enjoyed every moment of utilizing my strengths and believing I could truly do anything.

After this course, I then decided to study abroad in France, did a summer internship in New York City, came back to complete my last semester in college, bought a one-way ticket to New York City, and landed my dream job!

I understand that going to college isn't a possibility for every person and I recognize the privilege I had to leave my hometown. If college isn't a possibility, you can still expose yourself to people who are different than yourself if this is something you wish to do. Meeting people who have your dream job or even learning more about how your mentors got to where they can be a great first step. Just know you can do anything you set your mind to. There's always an opportunity waiting for those who prepare themselves through education (which can come in many forms) and then take action!

Hilary Hinrichs is a dedicated Nutrition Health Coach who helps empower busy professionals with weight loss, freeing them from anxiety, and having more energy! You can connect with her on her website http://www.holistichilary.com/, through Facebook at https://www.facebook.com/holistichilary or on Instagram at https://instagram.com/hilaryhinrichs

Unconditional Support

By Tonja D.

———

So many people have inspired me to do better. One of them is Charles, my husband. We got married young; he was only 18 and I was 19. I got pregnant before we married. I ended up in the hospital and had surgery to remove my gallbladder. He came to the hospital every day after work and was so patient with me. He often rubbed my back and was so loving with me.

After we were married, I wasn't doing well. When I grew up, my parents were part of a Satanic cult. I wouldn't wish the abuse I suffered as a child on anyone for any reason. I've struggled with severe mental health issues ever since. Charles was so patient with me, every step of the way. I went to the Center for Change for 3 months. He would come visit me as often as they allowed.

Along with mental health issues, I also suffered from opiates addiction. I think I started drugs to help me forget the abuse of my childhood. When that didn't work, I started self-mutilation. The pain in my mind seemed farther away when there was physical pain to focus on.

We moved when my oldest daughter was 12. I still struggled, yet Charles was always patient. Sometimes, I really couldn't understand why he stayed by me, considering everything I put him through.

In 2008, he fell and broke his back. I was finally stable with the help of medication and counseling, so I had started working at Walmart. Charles was in a brace. It hurt him to breathe, and he developed pneumonia. So, he ended up in the hospital for a couple of days.

He couldn't work so he applied for disability. It took a while, but he finally received SSI. We lost the house we were living in because we couldn't afford it and moved in with Charles's parents. Charles decided to apply for vocational rehabilitation and started going to school. He studied so hard and now he has one semester left.

Charles could have stayed on disability and lived like that for the rest of his life, yet he chose to work. He got a job designing the electrical and mechanical plans for car washes and other commercial buildings. His determination and patience have helped me to continue doing things like working, even when I'm in pain and it's hard.

Things haven't been the best for him, but he has persevered. Charles isn't perfect. None of us are. I've always wished we could go to church together. I keep praying he will one day go with me, and I often listen to church on my phone at work and try to be a good example for him. However, I know that even if Charles isn't religious, without him, I wouldn't have made it to the mental stability I currently have. Sometimes, the best thing we can do for someone else is just be there for them, and Charles has always stayed with me and been there when I needed him most.

Making Memories, Not Regrets

By Rosilee Barreto

———

I remember hearing this story in church as a teenager. I wish I could give credit to the person who told it, but, sadly, I don't remember who it was. I don't even know if it was a true story or not, but the moral of the story has stuck with me.

There once was a man named Larry who seemingly had it all. He had a loving wife and four loving children. He worked very hard to provide for his family. He wanted to create wealth and began making land investments on the side. Soon he found out that one of the properties he had invested in was highly sought after by commercial developers. He received offers to buy the land almost daily. Finally, he received an offer he couldn't resist and sold the property.

Larry was smart enough to invest the money he received from the property into an even bigger real estate venture. Soon, he was doubling his income every year and his life seemed to all of his friends and acquaintances to be a great success.

To his family, however, Larry was a constant failure. Larry's wife had only two requests for Larry no matter what big project he was working on: 1) That he be home for dinner so they could eat together as a family, and 2) that he take each of his children out to have one-on-one time at least once a week. Since they had four children, she thought he could easily take one child per week and spend at least 2 hours with that child, so that by the end of the month, he would have spent at least 2 hours of individual time with each child.

At first, Larry thought the requests were perfect. He appreciated that his wife would take care of everything else at home and only expected those two things. However, as time went on, and his successes got bigger, he realized that there was no way he could be home for dinner every night. He also had to keep rescheduling his one-on-one time with his children because he had to work around his clients' schedules, and that made his own schedule vary week to week.

Weeks passed, and then months. Larry became more and more addicted to his financial success. He was now doing motivational speaking gigs at least once a month for companies or individuals who wanted to learn his secrets for success.

One day, after a long flight from having given a motivational speech, he came home and found the house completely empty. He searched the house and couldn't find his wife or children anywhere. Finally, when he reached the kitchen, he saw a note on the fridge from his wife that simply said, "We're out making memories. Wish you could have come, but we couldn't wait anymore for you to be there to make memories with us."

Larry sat down at the bar stool in his kitchen and his eyes were drawn to the family calendar. There he saw that just that month, he had missed a basketball game from one son, a football game for another, a school play for one of his daughters, and a talent show that all four children had participated in.

Larry stood up and took the calendar down. He started reviewing past month's activities. Finally, he found an activity that he had been there for, a New Year's Day party with his in-laws. It was October, and the last family event he had been there for was at the beginning of January.

He looked around and saw the pictures of his children. It was like he was seeing them for the first time in a long time. They had all grown up so much.

Suddenly, he felt an immense regret for the time not spent with his family. He realized he had failed miserably at keeping the two requests his wife had asked of him. He had rarely made it home for dinner, and he hadn't spent hardly any time with his children.

Since his wife hadn't left an address where his family was or where to find them, Larry decided to use the time until they came home to make a new resolve to be a better husband and father. He called a local copy shop and had them make a banner for him that said, "Make Memories, Not Regrets," which he hung over his office door. He also had a smaller one made that he pinned to the visor of his car.

He then spent hours going through his finances and deciding what he would keep and what he would cut out to free up time for his wife and family. Of the four businesses he had, he realized that there was only one that he actually had to be involved in personally. For the other businesses, he could hire a general manager to run things for him.

He wrote out a new schedule for himself in which he could make it home every day for dinner and could make it to every upcoming event that his children had. He was even going to have extra time to have one-on-one time with each of them like his wife had requested.

When his family returned, Larry apologized to them and asked for their forgiveness. He then told them what he had done to arrange his schedule in a way that he could be there for them. His family was skeptical at first; they didn't think he would actually keep his word. However, after several weeks of Larry sticking to his plan, the family began to feel more united than they ever had before.

From then on, whenever anyone asked Larry what his secret to success was, he told them it was to, "Make Memories, not Regrets," and that the only way to live was to be there for the moments that truly matter, with the people who matter most.

Overcoming

By Destiny Kroeber

———

I'm the youngest of 5 children; I have 3 sisters and 1 brother. We have two amazing, hardworking parents who loved and cared for us with all their hearts. We didn't have a whole lot of material things when I was a kid, but I was truly blessed because I don't ever recall experiencing any feelings of insecurity in my family. We've always been and still are extremely close.

I was a pretty average kid. I liked to climb trees, play almost any sport, get dirty, and I loved animals. I also loved when my dad would bring me along on appliance repair jobs and teach me to use the tools. My mom also involved me in everything she did. My siblings were amazing and I looked up to all of them in different ways. I was never neglected for attention and always had someone around, even when my parents worked multiple jobs. I never, ever felt alone.

I was about 12 years old when I started smoking cigarettes by stealing them from my friend's parents.

Then I started stealing them from the gas station (back when a lot of gas stations kept a little plastic case of them on the counter up front). Sometimes, we'd even convince someone who was old enough to buy cigarettes for us. I tried alcohol for the first time at about 13, given to me by the older brother of a friend who told me if I kissed him, he'd let me have if for free. That was followed almost immediately by marijuana, which came from the same friend, who gave it to me for various "harmless" trades: a kiss, sometimes a hug, sometimes a "rub."

That went on for a while before I got introduced to cocaine. From that point on between the ages of 13 and 15, I was almost always high and would take or do any drug that was offered to me. I had grown accustomed to the fact that I would need to do a "trade" in order to get a hit. I started abusing and treating my family horribly. I stole from them. I physically and emotionally abused my mother when she tried to help me. I constantly fought my dad. Sometimes he would reach out to hug me and tell me he was there to help me, and I would end up screaming at him, calling him horrible names and one time I even spit in his face. I physically and emotionally abused my sisters. I skipped school almost daily, and when I did go, I went sky high on whatever drug I had at the time. I lied constantly, snuck out of the house regularly, and often didn't come home at all because I was too high to move, or in some cases, to even remember that I should go home. It was a rapid downward spiral all in a matter of just a few years. I chose to hang out with negative, abusive people. Very few of them I even considered actual "friends."

The first time I was raped, I wasn't quite 14 years old. I was at the house of a friend of a friend whom I'd never met. I was high and drunk but aware enough to say "no" and realize what was happening, but this turned out to be just part of the deal. I had been given the drugs for free, so now I had to give something back as a "trade." I began to understand that the value of my "trade" needed to inrease because of the value of the drugs I was getting. I realized this was going to be my new normal.

I ended up going out with the guy, who thoroughly convinced me (without actually saying specific words) that he didn't actually rape me. He had just claimed me as his girlfriend and that was what girlfriends "had" to do for their boyfriends, whether they wanted to or not. So that happened many times over the 8 months that I was his girlfriend. He also "lent" me out to his friends or people he needed drugs from. He was also the first boy who hit me. Often, this would happen because I approached him when he was upset about something else.

One time when crossing the road from school, I nearly got hit by a car because I was high and not paying attention. When I got to the other side, he punched me in the face because I scared him and should have paid closer attention. Most of the time, his reasons for hitting me were similar to that. He got arrested later that year on unrelated issues, and only then was I able to move forward.

The next chapter of my life was almost immediately after he was arrested: I started going out with another guy within the same circle of people. He was nice and funny and had a lot of drug connections. I had kind

28

of lost full understanding of what self-respect meant at that point, so I just allowed things and did things that continued to chip away at my self-esteem. I was 15 years old when I got pregnant with his child. I gained about 60 lbs during this pregancy, putting me over 200 lbs at 15.

There are many different experiences throughout my life that I believe have *saved* my life at that particular moment in time, and getting pregnant is one of them. My parents have said multiple times that they were pretty confident that I would have been dead or in prison within a year.

One of my first responses to finding out I was pregnant as a teenager was that obviously it wouldn't be good for the baby if I continued to do drugs. I had to stop cold turkey. It was SO horrible in the beginning. I actually continued to smoke cigarettes during the first few months of pregnancy because I genuinely believed I was going to die without drugs and that taking the "edge" off with SOMETHING would help. With a lot of family support and counseling (individual and group), I stayed "clean" and didn't do drugs while I was pregnant. I even quit smoking cigarettes after a few months.

I was 16 on the day I decided to put my son up for adoption. It was 11 days before his birth. I was blessed to spend two full days with him before I placed him in the arms of his forever parents. Even if I had all the time in the world, I don't think I could ever adequately express my feelings at the time I put my son in someone else's arms.

I spent the following months in the darkest, loneliest place I had ever experienced. Even though I had an amazing family who stuck by me through all the horrible things I'd done to them and put them through, I just wasn't in a good place within myself. My family was there constantly, offering love and support in any way they knew how. But even then, I couldn't escape the darkness. This was the first time I remember genuinely considering ending my life. I hadn't been prepared for the pain of giving away my child. All the "preparation" I thought I'd been doing (talking to other birth mothers in the same situation, going to my support group, etc.) felt almost completely useless at that point.

Nevertheless, I lived. Despite walking away from almost all of my friends in an attempt to stay clean, being constantly stalked and harrassed by people I once considered friends, I lived. We ended up moving about 50 miles north of where I'd grown up for a fresh start and I did well there. I got my GED because I couldn't emotionally handle being around other teenagers. I got a job and tried to stay busy. I was slowly learning to adapt to a "new normal."

Unfortunately, it was very easy for me to fall back into needing to numb my thoughts and found myself seeking the high again. It wasn't nearly as bad this time, so I think I justified it in my mind. My family and I had been through a lot together, so I was focused really hard on treating them as well as I could. I didn't want them to know I was back to getting high almost every day. But I couldn't help the downward spiral. I couldn't stop the dark feelings turning up again.

I had just turned 17 and started hanging out with the same type of people I had tried to leave behind. I found myself in worse and worse situations. One of these times, while high, I was raped again. I honestly think that my mind almost wanted it to happen. Like it was something that I knew would help me bury all the feelings and put on a tough face.

People used to tell me that time would heal all things and I quickly decided for myself that that saying was NOT true. Time didn't heal anything for me. I just learned to adapt to all of my pain. I adapted to all of my experiences. They became part of me, and I could either let that fact swallow me up or just accept it and move forward. Not move on, just forward.

A few months after I started getting deeper into depression, drugs, and self-harm, I met a guy. It's the sentence that started each chapter of my life, and each chapter before now had ended the same. However, this guy was different. I craved to be near him in a way I had never felt before. He was completely the opposite of every guy I had ever been around. I had ZERO desire for a relationship, but this guy was an amazing friend and the absolute best person to have entered my life. He had never done a drug in his entire life, he didn't demand sex from me, and he even taught me to stop saying, "I'm sorry" for every single thing that came out of my mouth. I quickly found myself *wanting* to be clean around him.

At first, I was only trying to be clean for him because I knew he wouldn't support my drug habit. Then, slowly, it turned into me seeing that I liked who I was around him and who I was when I was clean. I consider this another "moment in time." He saved my life. He still saves my life every day.

My reflexes of wanting that high when my brain spirals will always be there. Those thoughts are there EVERY moment in my life that feels even remotely

31

overwhelming. Every time I feel uncomfortable, anxious, scared, or mad, I want that high. But even at our worst, somehow I'm able to look at this man and be reminded why I choose to be clean. Every day, I choose. I've had to allow positive, healthy energy into my life in order to push the negative energy out. We've been together since 2003 and I've been completely clean since 2004. We've worked HARD to overcome our obstacles and deal with the things of my past that surface frequently. Every day, we choose to move forward in life together. His ethics and energy are what fuels me to want a positive life. I'm grateful he was there for me when I needed him most and that he continues to be there for me today.

Sometimes, all it takes is one person to believe in you for you to start moving mountains.

The Dream

By Tanya Cohen

'm riding in the passenger seat of my stepdad's truck and we're traveling down a dirt road. The land around us is bare and there isn't anything to see as far I can see. Just miles of emptiness surround us. The road begins to twist and turn, I can feel the bumps as we drive over rocks. I turned to my stepdad and ask him, where are we going? He doesn't answer but looks forward and nods his head to the front of us. I turned my focus back to the path we're traveling on, and, in the distance, there appears to be a house.

As we get closer, the day seems to get darker, I'm starting to have an uneasy feeling about this place. Then as if I blinked my eyes, we're suddenly there. My stepdad parks the truck and we both get out. He starts walking up to the metal gate that looks very old and falling apart. The path that leads up to the house is broken with overgrown weeds. As I follow my gaze up, the house doesn't look like anyone could be living here; it's very dark and creepy. Steps lead up to a wrap-around porch and some of the wood planks are broken. The house appears to be two stories, and by the broken windows, it has to be abandoned.

I just stand there at the gate and tell my stepdad not to go in there. The fear that filled me was growing, and it wasn't fear for me; it was for him. I had this overwhelming feeling that whatever was in this house was going to hurt him. So, I ran up to his side, avoiding the broken stones that could trip me and the broken steps that look to have no ending in the darkened holes. I get to his side, he looks down at me, nods his head, turns to face the door, and knocks three times.

No one answers at first, then the door slowly creaks open into darkness. There doesn't appear to be anyone there. As we step inside, the day also becomes dark outside. I'm holding my stepdad's hand now and waiting for something, I feel like I've been here before and that I left something important here. A small flicking light starts to come out of the darkness from inside the house. Someone is carrying a candelabra. He's very tall, dressed all in black, and wearing the tallest top hat I've ever seen. I ask him, "What do you want?" He points at my stepdad and says one word, "Him." I look at my stepdad and tell him to run, to get out. This is when the front door slams shut, and my stepdad is gone; he just vanishes. The man in black lets out a loud evil laugh and I scream!

I'm covered in sweat; my heart is pounding as I'm sitting in bed, and I guess I screamed myself awake. I had it again, the reoccurring dream I've had for two years ever since learning of my dad's death in a motorcycle accident around the same time my mom came home from having brain surgery for her cancer treatment. See, my mom had remarried, and he was a really good person. As a nine-year-old little girl, though, I didn't know how to process the loss of my dad that day, the relief of getting my mom back, and then this other man trying to be my dad.

It was the middle of the night, and my grandma came running into my room. I was staying with my paternal grandparents over the summer that year. She put her arms around me as I sat there shaking and crying. She had asked me what was wrong as she was rocking me and trying to calm me down. We stayed like this until I was able to let the fear subside. She then asked me again if I was able to talk about it. I was calmer now, and the dream was starting to fade, but the memory of this dream was always present. I hadn't been able to tell my mom about this dream in detail but, in this moment, I was able to share it with my grandma. She listened to every detail until I was completely done. Then I said with tears in my eyes, "Grandma, I don't know what to do. Every time I close my eyes, this dream starts all over again."

She looked at me and said, "What we need to do is pray, let's ask God to help guide you and be by your side." So, we both sat there and prayed. I can't remember all of the words she said in the prayer, but I do remember feeling stronger and more powerful. So much so, that I felt better when we were done and was able to lay back down and try to get some sleep. Grandma told me that she loved me, knew what a brave girl I was, and that God would be with me even though I couldn't see him; he would be by my side especially when I needed him the most.

I closed my eyes as she left the room. I fell asleep and began dreaming the same dream. Although I'm back in my dream again, something is different this time: I'm aware.

The dream starts the same, with me riding in my stepdad's truck and walking toward the house. However, once we're inside the house, the dream changes.

The man in black is pointing at the vacant space my stepdad was standing in, but I'm not screaming. I look at this evil man and demand that he give me my dad back. He stops laughing and his black eyes just stare at me for a few moments. He then tells me that in order to save my dad, I had to find the thing I lost. He then points to the old falling-apart stairs that lead up to the second floor. Then he vanishes.

I'm terrified but still feel strong in a determined way, I've never felt this sense of courage before, which was strange because I never left this room before and now, I'm going to go deeper into the house. I'm not leaving here without my family! Like in the movies the stairs seem to keep going and going and once I finally make it to the top, there's a closed door at the end of a long hallway. But what's interesting about this door is that light is coming from the bottom; it's the only light to be seen. In that moment, I feel that what's behind this door is very important to me. I start to walk toward it, but it keeps getting further away, so I started running. Just as I'm getting winded, the door starts to get closer. I have a sense of relief; I'm going to see what's behind this door. It's suddenly very important.

I make it to the door, and now I'm terrified to open it. I take a couple deep breaths and hear a baby's giggle, so I put my hand on the door handle and turn it. The door begins to open into a blinding light; I have to put my hand over my eyes so I can start to focus on the images that are hard to make out. As my eyes adjust to the light, sitting on the floor are my mom, stepdad, and baby brother. My family is here, the relief I'm feeling is overwhelming, but just then it's replaced with fear. The evil force I sensed before is coming down the hall toward us, toward my family! I looked at their smiling faces, completely unaware of the evil that's coming for them, scream "NO!" and slammed the door closed, leaving them inside in the light. I turn around and scream at the evil forces that they can't have my family and that I'm going to stop them.

I'm now standing in what looks like the kitchen, and the man in black with the top hat is staring at me, he seems to be even taller now, and he has a creepy companion next to him. I'm staring back into his evil black eyes. He tells me that I can't have them and that they're his. A boiling sensation of rage spills out of me and I suddenly have a lightsaber in my right hand. I grip it with both hands and swing it through the man in black and his companion. They disappear in black smoke. The room starts to feel calmer, and I realize I still have my family to rescue. As I walk around the corner, I hear a sound behind a brick wall. Something is in there, and the bricks are starting to move. I hear a faint sound of someone saying, "Help me." The bricks are becoming looser, so I start to take them off the wall one at a time. There IS someone in here, so I start removing them faster. It's a little girl. I help her out and ask her who she is, she looks to be about six years old. She points at me, and I realize in this moment that this is ME. I was locked away in fear and pain for so long since my dad's death. In that moment, in my dream, I have just saved myself, the thing I had lost. All I can do is hug her, and as I begin to cry, I tell her she's safe now, we're safe now.

It was morning when I woke up and I was smiling. I looked up at the ceiling and thanked God for helping me. Then I remember my grandma and how she helped me last night. I went to find her in the kitchen making my favorite eggs. I ran up to her and hugged her so tight, then started to tell her about my battle with the devil.

I never had the dream again after that night. When I say it was a reoccurring dream, I mean it plagued me almost every night for a couple years. My grandma believed in me when I was scared and helped me find a belief in God, even when I was scared and lost. I'll forever be grateful to her for loving me enough and not just dismissing a little girl's crazy dream. She helped me to find the courage so that I could find the scared little girl I metaphorically hid behind a bricked-up wall in a scary old, abandoned house when I didn't know how to process my grief. I also realized a few years later that I was keeping my family locked away in a safe place because I was afraid to lose anyone else.

I believe that, in life, if something isn't happening directly to us, we can sometimes just brush off a situation as a "don't worry; this will pass," "time heals," "you'll get over it," or, in my case, "it's just a dream." It takes a special person to acknowledge when someone is truly hurting and, instead of just patting them on the head, sit with them and give them support and reassurance that you believe in them. Belief in another person and a higher power is a force to be reckoned with. It makes a person truly able to do anything, even find themselves again.

In memory of Grandma Behel.

Doors

By JoLyn Brown

November 2014

The last glimpse I take of LuAnn Staheli is while I'm standing in the hallway at the top of the stairs, looking back into the room she's dying in. I've been there an hour and other friends have arrived to visit with her. I know it's time to leave—I've said goodbye—but I stop at the door.

LuAnn used to stand outside her classroom as I arrived for her Jr. High English class. In my strongest memory, she wears a red silk shirt. She knows something is wrong even before I reach her. She asks me what happened, and tears spill down my face.

Two things are tangled up in my fourteen-year-old mind. The night before, I'd written my very first complete short story: thirteen pages. It was due the next day. After midnight, just as I'd tapped in the last line, the computer crashed, and I lost half of the story. Worse, I was woken not long after going to bed by the hushed and urgent voice of my mom, "Uncle Greg has died." I spent the rest of the night in the living room with my siblings, waiting for my parents to return from my aunt's house.

LuAnn comforted me about my uncle's death. She told me it was okay that I only had half a paper to turn in. "Write it again," she told me. "The second time is better anyway."

At the top of the stairs nearly fourteen years later, I recognize the last room she'll greet me from. I hesitate, even as I hear her talking to her new visitors. I look back and try to memorize something, something to hold the way I hold the memory of a red silk shirt. I intend to sneak a last glance—she won't ever know—instead, she meets my eyes. We both stay like that, eyes locked. Later, I won't remember what she wore, or even what color the blanket over her was. All I will remember is that she saw me.

When I get to the bottom of the stairs, her husband meets me.

I try to stay positive. "I'm glad I came. It was good to see her."

"She's not going to live," he says. "Did she tell you that? The cancer is killing her."

Something crushes in my chest. "I know."

I've never met him before. I've never been to LuAnn's house. I don't even know his name, but I wrap my arms around him, and he cries on me.

LuAnn didn't cry. She didn't dwell on the ending when we visited. She talked to me about writing books. LuAnn didn't hug me. Touching was too painful for her. I hold her husband instead, the way I would have wanted to hug LuAnn. Not only because of the day I cried in her classroom but also because she's part of the things inside me that are good. She's the spark that relit my dreams, the voice that I hear when I write. She's part of the reason I'm about to publish my first book, a book she will never read.

May 2010

I stand in the line of wanna-be authors at my first ever Storymakers Conference in Provo, Utah. I'm a single speck in a sea of people and I don't even know for sure what to say when someone asks me what I write. When I tell them about the story I'm working on, I sense something is missing in the plot, a vital part I've yet to pin down. I'm pretty much a fraud. After checking in, I cross to the sitting area, and I freeze. I recognize her back, the way her hair falls to her shoulders, the way she leans over a book she's reading. *It's Mrs. Staheli!*

I approach like a nervous teenager, even though I'm married and have a kid of my own. What do I call her? What if she doesn't remember me?

She lifts her head and sees me. "JoLyn!"

I'm startled and a familiar sense of warmth fills me.

I go to her class. When I hear her teach, it's like the source of all my writing knowledge has been located. Her voice has been in my head all these years, and I didn't even realize it. Later, she'll tell me she's available if I need a mentor to read my story and give me feedback.

I get her email address. I buy all her books. I have her sign them. I keep writing.

August 2017

The doctor swallows hard. Her voice is strained. "No, I really think you need to head to the ER. It will be the fastest way to get admitted to the hospital."

My husband, Jacob, shakes his head. I know he's thinking about the expense, but I've finally read in the doctor's face the things she isn't saying. The scans of Jacob's stomach are worse than she's let on. Whatever's wrong is something she's seen before. I can tell it's bad. She's more worked up than we are.

"Please go to the ER," she says again.

I touch my husband's arm. "I think you should go."

He still shakes his head. It takes a several minutes longer to convince him. A few days later, the doctors make the diagnosis official.

Cancer

October 2017

The hollow parking garage echoes as I make my way toward the hospital. The days are blurred, the time a haze. Jacob's been in and out of the hospital. He's had blood transfusions, PICC lines, drain lines, and chemo. Now he's in the ICU again and I don't know how long this will go on. I don't even know if he will live. As I reach the entrance to the garage, the sunlight spills into the darkness around me, and I feel an invisible someone beside me. I recognize her, the sense of her, the feeling of an angel person walking side by side with me. Her name comes to my mind, *LuAnn*. I take a deeper breath and know God sent her to me.

May 2018

When I pick up the groceries, it's nearly eight P.M. A young girl loads them in, and I help her. She tells me she writes fan fiction. *Prep for Storymakers Conference,* I think. Tomorrow, I'll have this "what do you write?" conversation a hundred times.

I drive home on the artificial high of knowing I have no time and much to do. It buries the guilt. A little. I've been planning on going to this conference for months. Months that should have gotten Jacob to a place where he could watch the kids. Instead, he's in the ICU again. I don't know how to make all the ends meet. Who will be with Jacob when I'm not? Who will be with the kids when I'm not? My mother-in-law is here, but she can only be in one place. I'm going to have to ask her to stay with the kids, leaving Jacob alone in the hospital.

By the time I crawl into an empty bed, Jacob's mom has arranged for an aunt to visit him tomorrow. My clothes are set out, my kids taken care of. I'm supposed to be excited. I think I am. Somewhere inside. If I can only dig down to it.

Things are tight the next morning when I oversleep—tighter when my mother-in-law comes up stairs with her computer, near tears because she can't connect to her mandatory meeting. She and I are twin stressors, both near breaking. I can't fix the computer. I can't fix most things lately. Good intentions are my daily results. I leave thirty minutes late.

I turn the music up in the car and then turn it up again. I take deep breaths. I can't stop the sinking panic inside me. I'm on the board of directors for the Storymakers Guild. This year my responsibilities will be different. What I want more than anything is to be helpful and make a good impression, but I'm already late. And an hour away, my husband is waking up in the ICU.

"Heavenly Father, please help me calm down." God can send me an angel. I both want and need an angel now. A name skips across my rushing mind. *LuAnn.*

Can I ask God to send me her? Before I even finish thinking it, I know I can.

Not only would she be the perfect companion but also I think she'd like to come to the Storymakers conference again. If I'm with LuAnn, I can do anything. *"Please send me Mrs. Staheli."*

The sense of an arm wrapping over my shoulders settles on me and the anxiety leaves like a wind has blown through. It's so immediate, I cannot doubt she's there. I don't have to explain anything about what I'm going through to her. She already knows. I park and walk to the building with my head high. I can do this.

LuAnn is with me when I walk through the door.

JoLyn Brown was raised alongside a peach orchard where she worked with her family. Some of her favorite memories are of listening to stories told by her relatives. These stories and her own experiences provide inspiration for her writing. She's published two contemporary teen novels and four non-fiction faith based books. JoLyn is currently working on a novella for readers of her teen books and a fantasy novel. You can connect with her at www.jolynbrown.com.

Choosing to Be Healthy

By Destiny Kroeber

———

When I was 15, I got pregnant. I had been into drugs and my pregnancy was hard, emotionally and physically. I gained about 60 lbs. My baby was about 7 pounds when he was born, so I think after he was born, I lost 7 pounds of that 60. I was never a small or super thin girl, but I had never considered myself *fat* either. However, after my pregnancy, giving my baby up for adoption, and mental spiraling, I gained weight almost nonstop.

In 2012, during a different pregnancy, I gained about 50 pounds. I was diagnosed with gestational diabetes and without going into every single detail, it was a really scary experience for my partner and me. No matter what we tried to do, it didn't seem to make a difference. At 37 weeks of pregnancy, the doctor insisted that I be induced with the warning that our baby could be stillborn. The NICU crew was in the room when I gave birth, ready to take her away. Miraculously, she was born healthy and strong, with almost no problems.

We were really blessed, but I'll never forget how scary that felt.

On the day after she was born, I was 301 pounds. Because of how uncontrollable my gestational diabetes was, my doctor and diabetes specialist had warned me that there was about a 99% chance that I would develop Type 2 diabetes. In September of 2015, when we went to the doctor to discuss trying for another baby, my diagnosis of Type 2 diabetes was official.

After this diagnosis came my first REAL push to get healthy. I remember thinking that I needed to get HEALTHY, not just "lose weight," especially since "health" now had a new view for me. Throughout my years of obesity, I had tried a ton of different approaches to losing weight. Sometimes, I was successful and lost some weight, but it wouldn't be long before I gained it all back.

I joined a casual fitness group on Facebook that a friend of mine ran and invited me to join. There were some fitness challenges given each day, some ranging between doing a certain amount of jumping jacks per day to daily tips to eat healthier. One of the daily challenges that popped up one day was to start using daily affirmations. We were challenged to say outloud in the mirror a simple affirmation, "I accept myself unconditionally right now."

It sounded simple enough, to just go to the mirror and say that affirmation outloud. However, the first time I went to the mirror with that challenge, I cried at my reflection and I couldn't say it out loud no matter how hard I pushed myself. I could barely even say it in my head. I failed the challenge that day. And the next day, and the next day. It took me at least a week before

I could even FAKE it enough to say that affirmation out loud. But I finally convinced myself that if I could do nothing else, I could at least TRY every single day, and I was going to THINK hard about what those words really meant. I think the problem for me with that phrase is that not only did I have to look at my body and try to accept it as it was, I also looked INTO myself to who I was on the inside. Then I would think, "How could I POSSIBLY accept all of *this* as it is?!" All of my thoughts and feelings were attacking me, and I didn't like anything about the person I was looking at in the mirror.

So I decided to try something else. I decided to write down the affirmation so I could just look at the words. Then after reading the words, I would force myself to find something that I liked about myself. Just one thing I was good at, or a nice thought I had about myself. Soon, I could say the affirmation out loud, and truly believe it. I could even say it with a smile on my face!

Once I truly started to believe this, that I genuinely accepted that girl in the mirror, my entire outlook on my life began to improve. I realized that it's not like I can get away from that girl in the mirror. And if I can't get away from her, I might as well get to know her!

Keep in mind that throughout this process, I was checking in with this positive support group DAILY. Part of the magic of the group was just having somewhere to voice how I was feeling, and then having positive support from people saying things like, "It's okay to feel the way you're feeling." I didn't need people to feed into my self pity, or to tell me it was okay, or that things would get better. I simply wanted someone to say, "Your feelings are valid. You're allowed to feel the way that you feel-the good, the bad, and the ugly."

Most people are familiar with a certain phrase mentioned in the recovery world (therapy, rehab, groups, etc.) that recovering addicts often get clean "for" someone else. I can't tell you how many times I've heard someone say, "I want to get clean for my kids," or "for my family." Following this same mindset, I began to look for someone I could be healthy "for" who would motivate me more than just trying to motivate myself.

The perfect opportunity came during the beginning part of the fitness challenge group that I was in. My husband was told by the doctor that he had really high blood pressure as well as sleep apnea and it was probably mostly, if not all, due to his weight. At that moment, health became a priority for someone other than myself. I wanted HIM to be healthy. Since I was the one preparing family meals, he asked me if I could keep his meals down to 1,500 calories per day. I decided this would be a goal for me as well. I had never cared how much my husband weighed, and he had never cared how much I weighed (and I'm significantly bigger than him!), but reading all of the facts about sleep apnea and high blood pressure made me put his health first as a priority. That became my goal, to help my husband get healthy.

After all of my years of failing at becoming healthier, it wasn't until my husband was alongside me that I was finally successful. *WE* were successful. He lost almost 90 pounds, was able to trash his sleep apnea machine, and was approved to be completely off BP medication.

As my husband continued on his journey for better physical health, I became more focused on positive mental health. I didn't plan that, but I realized because of all of the negative experiences of my past, a negative attitude kept holding me back. I decided that without a healthy mind, I couldn't have a healthy body, at least not the type of health I wanted to have and KEEP.

I started really fousing on my mind and what had piled up inside my head to make me feel the way I did about myself. I knew I could make the physical reflection of myself change in the mirror, but my reflection on the inside was never going to change unless I did something about it.

A good challenge for my mind came during my kickboxing workouts. My sister had gotten me into kickboxing when we were younger, and I found myself drawn to the sport for my workouts. Even though I had done it before, I constantly struggled with my mind telling me I couldn't do it, that it was too hard. In the beginning, I couldn't even get 10 minutes into the workout before I felt like I was going to puke. I'd often reach my point of exhaustion and then stop, frustrated with my body and frustrated that my mind wasn't strong enough to overcome mental limits.

Then a friend of mine started saying, "I can do hard things" to herself daily. I liked the mantra and started saying it to myself ANY time I felt frustrated about my limits, whether it was a frustrating parenting moment, doing a task and failing at it, or during a workout when I felt I couldn't go any further. I started saying it outloud whenever any feelings of frustration or doubt would surface. I started saying it to my daughter whenever she would say she couldn't do something or get frustrated. I said it so much, apparently, that soon every time I would appear to be struggling (like when I was huffing and puffing and sweat was flying everywhere), my daughter would say to me, "You can do hard things, Mommy!" Talk about motivation! I realized I was capable of a lot more than I thought whenever I used the phrase "I can do hard things." I would highly recommend that mantra to anyone facing a hard challenge.

The affirmation "I accept myself unconditionally right now" is still on the wall in my bathroom. I put it in a place where I HAVE to look at it every day. Learning to accept and LOVE myself has been one of the hardest things I've done for myself. The affirmation "I can do hard things" is right next to it. Because part of accepting myself is also believing that I can do hard things.

People have congratulated me and commented that I've worked so hard, and that must be why the weight has come off. It's true that I have worked hard, but exercising and positive food choices have NOT been the challenging part of my weightloss journey. The most challenging part of my journey has been learning to respect and love my body and mind. I realized something one day while standing in front of my mirror. A thought came to my mind, "My body is my home and I will not tear it down." This is the same body I was born with. It's the same body that has been with me thoughout everything I've experienced in life. It has been physically weak and physically strong. It has been raped, beaten, stretched, and abused in many ways. It has also built human beings. And it doesn't matter whether it's big or small, stretched out or not, strong or weak, it's the house that I live in, and I want to be comfortable in my home.

This has been an absolutely amazing process for me in every way, especially mentally. Without a doubt, my successes have come from positive support in everyday life, learning to love myself and accept myself as I am without focusing on the scale or other people's opinions of me.

Achieving my goal of being healthy has resulted in losing over 100 pounds and a combined total of 38 inches. In the process, I've gained so much. I can run and play with my kids. I can sit on a swing or go down a slide. I can run 5ks. I can truly take care of this body I love.

If I could say anything to someone struggling with getting healthy, it's this: "You're worth it! And you can do it because you can do hard things. The road will not be easy, and you'll need positive people to support you, but you can do it. Choose to accept the challenge of good health. It will bless your life in more ways than you can possibly imagine. You can do it!"

Helping a Stranger

By Rosilee Barreto

―――――――――

In my early adult years, I had the privilege of traveling to a different state for a service mission for my church. Each day, we would do some form of service, whether it be painting houses or fences, volunteering at the food bank, or simply talking to people about God and what faith in Him can do. Some days, when we didn't have an actual service activity planned, we would go out and just talk to people in the park or ask people if we could help them with anything, like take out the garbage or help carry groceries. We always served in pairs, as it was far less awkward to talk to strangers when there were two of us than trying to talk to others on your own. In our mission lingo, we called the other person we served with a "companion."

One day my companion and I had made a goal to speak to EVERY person we saw. As we were walking from a park, she saw a man sitting in his car with his eyes closed. She started walking to the car, and I said,

"Hey! He's sleeping. Leave him alone." She reminded me of our goal that morning and said that since she had seen him, she was going to knock on the window. She knocked, and the man's eyes flew open. He looked very surprised as he rolled down the window and my companion said, "Well, good morning, sir. We were wondering if we could share a short message about Jesus Christ." The man started crying. We were confused and waited, until he finally collected himself enough to say that his wife had died three days before. He was sitting in his car trying to decide if his life were worth living without her. He had just told God that if He didn't send a sign in the next five minutes, he was going to take his own life....and then there we were knocking on his window wanting to talk to him about Jesus. He said that he knew that God was telling him that he could keep on living without his wife and that he would be okay. He thanked us for knocking on his window, then started his car, and drove away.

That experience taught me that if you make a goal, you should follow through, no matter what. I was more than willing to not follow through with our goal because I thought that I would inconvenience someone or get yelled at. However, my not following through with our goal to talk to every person we saw could have resulted in someone else ending their life because they thought no one cared.

Sometimes, people are placed in our path based on what our goals are for the day. If we put off a certain thing we're scared of doing or not sure how to do, such as a phone call or an in-person visit, we might just find out later that the other person was waiting for someone to reach out.

That day in the park, I learned that if you have a gut feeling that you should do something, you should just do it, without questioning why. It may turn out horribly awkward or less than desirable...but it could also turn out great! You never know. So instead of always wondering what would or could happen, just do it! Whatever your main goal is for the day, decide to do it first. You may be surprised how many changes take place in your life by doing first the thing you'd rather put off until later or not do at all. You might even save someone's life, maybe even your own.

The Unexpected Painter

As told by Richard Davis and Darlene Nelson. Some excerpts also taken from the book PLACE OF PROMISE.

The story of Jack Thomas is a compilation of many miracles. At the age of five, Jack became the victim of Muscular Dystrophy. He was handicapped according to the world's values but not to Jack himself. He turned his stumbling blocks into stepping stones. *

Born into a farming community in the 1940s, life for Jack wasn't easy. In those days, houses, stores, and community places weren't equipped with handicap access. There were no sidewalks or wide doors, meaning the use of a wheelchair wasn't an option outside of the house. If Jack wanted to go somewhere, he had to call a friend or neighbor to give him a ride on their back.

In those days, most of the members of his community farmed to make ends meet. Jack's family, friends, and neighbors would join together to help each other during planting and harvesting seasons. He would see others out in their fields working from sunrise to sunset. However, Jack was usually confined to his house. He had almost no use in his legs, and his arms were only half functional. One of his arms he could move up and down at the shoulder joint but had no function in the fingers to be able to grip anything. His other arm couldn't move, but his fingers were able to grip and hold items. In order for him to eat, he had to use both arms: one hand to hold the eating utensil and then the other arm to lift the first arm up to get the food to his mouth.

Since Jack couldn't help with the farming, he decided to find a different way to be useful to his family and community; he started to paint.

With one hand, he would hold the paint brush, and with the other arm, he would move the hand gripping the paintbrush to perform the brush strokes.

It was painfully slow, and sometimes it would take Jack weeks or months to finish a painting. Each painting he finished he would give to someone in the community who had done something kind for him. His paintings became well-known and cherished to many families. One painting in particular took Jack months to complete. It was such a beautiful painting that several members of the community requested that the painting be hung in the community church for all to see.

In addition to Jack's painting, he called members of the community on a daily basis. He would usually just call to chat and see how everyone was doing. If he found out that someone needed help, he would call another member of community and ask them to go help the person in need. If that person said they couldn't or wouldn't help, Jack would say, "All right then. Guess I'll have to go do it myself." Knowing that Jack would probably try to go help the person in need, because that was just how he was, he would normally hear the response back, "No, Jack, that's alright. I'll make time to do what you've asked."

Jack also became an expert on the Ham radio. He started to talk to people all over the world. One day, when Richard Davis was at Jack's house, Jack introduced him to one of his friends in Japan. To Jack, everyone was his friend. There wasn't a person in the community who wasn't touched by Jack's kindness, either through his words or through his paintings.

It got to the point that members of the community would forget that Jack was handicapped until someone new moved to town. The new guy would say something like, "Oh, you mean the handicapped guy?" To which anyone listening would say, "We don't have a handicapped guy. We have Jack. We carry him on our backs when he needs it, but, usually, he's the one carrying us, lifting our spirits, and helping us soar." Jack never saw himself as handicapped, so it was easy for others to not see him that way either.

In the 1970s, the church where Jack's painting was held unexpectedly burst into flames. Members of the community rushed to get everything out of the church that they could while the fire was still burning bright. At the risk of their own lives, three men ran into the burning building to get Jack's painting and got out literally seconds before that section of the building collapsed.

When the new church building was finished, the first painting back in the building was Jack's painting, where it still hangs to this day. A shining tribute to a wonderful man who refused to be labeled by the world's standards. Where others may have made excuses because of physical limitations, Jack created a legacy that is still cherished to this day.

Place of Promise, page 177, article written by Verna Throckmorten.

Buying the Jersey

Name Withheld

I grew up with a burning desire to do a lot of things. I wanted to play competitive sports. I wanted to study something that would make me a millionaire. I wanted to have the most beautiful girlfriend on the block. I just wanted it all...but decided to start with sports.

I tried out for soccer the first year I was old enough. I made the team, but had to pay for my jersey in order to play. I went to my dad to ask for the money and he laughed at me. He told me we were in Mexico; every kid wanted to be a soccer star, but it was never going to happen and I might as well stop dreaming now.

Each time I tried out for another team, it was the same story. I couldn't get a job on my own because I had to help with the family business, and my dad would rather spend any extra money he had on beer. Several times, I begged my dad to buy me a jersey, but he refused. So, I could never play on the team.

My dad wasn't a bad guy; he just didn't care. He was too burned out from his own failed dreams. He was a butcher, and because our family needed the money, my brothers and I learned to be butchers as well. I learned how to work hard, but not how to enjoy life. I began to resent life in Mexico. I wanted a new life.

I came to the United States in 2001, one month before the twin towers fell. My brother had come to the United states first, and he had paid for me to come. Now I had to pay him back. I didn't speak a lick of English, so my first few jobs were based on following my brother around. I worked as a dishwasher, then a delivery boy, then a cook. I actually started doing pretty well for myself.

I got an apartment and invited my parents to come visit. Just after they came, I started talking to a girl online. Since I worked two jobs, it was hard to go out and meet people. This girl was in Mexico. I'll call her Maria. We started chatting about music, something I love. I found out she loved all of the same music that I did. She told me that all of her life, she had dreamed of seeing the United States. So I paid for her to get her visa and come visit.

I was very excited when she first got here. She was very pretty, and I thought that since I couldn't have my first two goals as a kid of playing sports or being rich, at least I could have a beautiful girlfriend.

At first, things were great. We got along, and she was kind toward my parents. Little by little, however, she wanted me to spend more and more time exclusively with her. If my parents wanted me to take them somewhere, Maria would get upset and convince me to stay home with her. Soon my parents decided to leave and go back to Mexico. I wasn't spending any time with them, and they didn't speak the language enough to do anything on their own. To this day, I still regret letting them leave like that.

Little by little, this woman started chipping away at my self-esteem. I couldn't go anywhere or do anything without her getting upset. Finally, after 6 months, I told her I was done, that she needed to go back to Mexico. She did…only to show up 3 months later and tell me she was pregnant with my child. She told me I had to marry her, because if her parents found out that she had a child out of wedlock, she would be disowned. She told me she didn't love me, but begged me to marry her to save her good name.

I didn't want to marry her, but I also didn't want to ruin her life. I also wanted to be there to see my kid. I made a goal as soon as I knew about the baby that I wanted to be a different dad than I had grown up with. I wanted to to be there for my kid. I wanted to support his or her goals. I wanted to pay for the jersey.

Shortly after we were married, things got crazy. Maria started telling me the baby wasn't mine and that she wanted nothing to do with me. I couldn't figure out why she had wanted to marry me if the baby wasn't mine. I asked her to go do a blood test. I wanted to know if it was true or not .

She came back and said the baby was mine, but that didn't mean anything. As soon as the baby was born, she was leaving. She actually did leave shortly after my son was born. She went to Mexico, and then I didn't know where she went for a while. She just showed up at my door about six months later and said that she had been wrong, that she missed me, and if I could take her back.

I did, because I wanted to be a good dad. I wanted to spend time with my son. I had a dream that maybe we could figure this out and be a family together. But the more I tried to do everything right, the more she thought I was doing everything wrong.

She asked me one day if I wanted more kids. I told her no. She said that was fine and that she would get on birth control. Three months later, she was pregnant. She had lied to me. During her second pregnancy, she went crazy. I don't know if it was the hormones or what. She started to refuse to let me help with my son. I couldn't change his diapers or give him a bath or she would accuse me of sexual abuse. She would go back and forth between being loving and kind, and then distant and angry.

One night she asked me to watch my son so she could go out. My brother came over and he and I started watching a movie. My son was in the crib next to us playing with some toys. When Maria got home and saw that my son wasn't asleep yet, she went berserk. She started jumping on the bed and screaming at me. I grabbed her arm and pulled her down. I told her to stop making a scene in front of my brother. She got even more angry and started pulling on my arm to force me to get out of the bed. I stood up, and she pulled harder. I twisted my arm to get out of her grip, and she fell back into the TV pretty hard. She then started crying and ran out of the room.

About a week later, I found out that she had put domestic violence charges against me for what happened that night. We went to court and the judge asked her if we were still living together. She said yes, and the judge said that all of the charges would be dropped then. If the situation wasn't bad enough for her to leave, then it wasn't bad enough.

After that, I didn't trust her at all about anything. It didn't help that she would constantly lie. When I would catch her in her lies, she always had an excuse. And then an excuse for her excuse. I wanted to leave, but then I found out we were having a little girl. I thought about that little girl, and I just couldn't leave.

One day she called me up and said that something was wrong with the baby and I needed to take her to the hospital immediately. I said she'd just have to figure it out because I was working. I was a manager at a restaurant at the time. It was very hard for me to just pick up and leave when everything in the store depended on me. And honestly, I was 100 percent sure she was lying and just wanted attention.

However, a couple of hours later, she called again to say that the doctors were taking the baby out. She still had three months until the due date. I didn't believe her and asked to talk to a doctor. She was super angry and told me if I wasn't going to believe her, then I couldn't come to the birth. By then, I could hear doctors and nurses talking and telling her it was time to go. I realized she had been serious. I rushed to the hospital, but by that time they wouldn't let me in. They told me that Maria had given specific instructions that she didn't want me there and that I would have to wait. By the time I saw Maria, I apologized and told her I would make it up to her. I drove her to the hospital every day so we could see our daughter in the NICU.

The day I finally got to hold my daughter was a day I will never forget. She was so small, she could fit in the palm of my hand. I had a strong desire to be there for her, to watch her grow up and be strong and healthy. I told Maria that our daughter was absolutely beautiful. She just looked at me and said, "Just remember that you didn't want her. When I asked you if you wanted more kids, you said no. When she's older, I will tell her you didn't want her." Somehow, this time, I knew that Maria wasn't lying.

It was actually a very happy day for the whole family when we could bring our daughter home from the hospital. My son loved her already and wanted to hold her all of the time. They were very cute. Maria was even in a really good mood. We had gotten along all day. After the kids went to bed, we started to get intimate. I suddenly blurted out, "Wait, you're on the pill again, right?" She glared at me, said that of course she was, and then we continued.

Two months later I found out she was pregnant again. This time, the only one I could blame was myself. I felt like an idiot for believing her. It felt like every time I believed her, she had been lying, and when I didn't believe her, she was telling the truth. It was a hellish cycle with no escape. Her hormones made her crazy again, to the point that I actually feared for my other children when I left for work. I was working three jobs now, trying to pay the bills and keep up with everything. I had extra bills now, as Maria had taken credit cards out in my name and maxed them out. Which meant I had to work a lot…and I had to leave my children with her alone a lot. I think that was the hardest part for me. Wondering if my kids would be there when I got back home.

The day before Maria went into labor with our third child, she and I had a huge fight. She accused me of never helping her, of never wanting this child, of not wanting to be a dad. She said I stayed away all of the time because I didn't want to be there with the kids. I was so angry. The whole reason I was working so hard was for the kids. I wanted them to be taken care of. It was expensive where we were living, and since I didn't have an American high school diploma or college education, it was hard to find high paying jobs. I was already at my max, and we were still just scraping by.

At the climax of our fight, I told her that if she really wanted this kid so bad, then she would have to take care of him herself. If what I was doing wasn't good enough for her, then she would have to find a way on her own. I saw something flash in her eyes, like she'd just had an idea. I regretted saying that in an instant. I didn't know what lay ahead of us, but I knew I wouldn't like it.

The next day she had our third child. I wasn't invited to the birth.

I decided after that to just focus on work and the kids. I would work all day, and then make sure I always had a treat or a gift in my hands when I came home. My kids loved that. They would come running to the door every day to see what I had brought them that day. That became my only reward for working so hard, to see my kids come running for me when I opened the door.

Maria started to hate that. She felt like she was home with them all day, and all they could talk about was when daddy would get home. She started keeping the kids in the back room, or taking them for walks when she knew I was coming home. She didn't want them to run to me or be excited to see me. I told her if she didn't want to be home all day, then she should get a job. We could rotate. I could work at night and she could work during the day. That way we could both see the kids, and the bills would still be paid. She said she was on board, and even found a job, but only held it for about 3 days. This kept happening over and over. So I kept working, only now I no longer had the satifisfaction of seeing my kids run to me at the door.

A few years went by, and I started staying away more and more. Anything I tried to do or buy for the kids would "mysteriously" disappear. I could do nothing right at home. So I started to go to bars with friends from work. I would come home drunk so I would be numb enough to not have to listen to Maria tell me how horrible I was. Finally, after about a year of that, I decided we needed a break from each other and from this horrible routine I hated and resented. A friend asked if I would go work with him for 3 months across the country. I jumped on it. I told Maria that I would be back in 3 months, and I would pay all of the bills while I was gone.

I sent Maria money every month to pay the rent and buy food. I was actually starting to miss her. The time spent away from her and the kids was harder than I thought it would be. One day just before the three months were up, I called to tell Maria that I was actually really excited to see her. Our time apart had made me realize I wanted to do things differently and that I would be there for her more. She listened, and then told me that she wanted a divorce and hung up.

I left the next day. I didn't even wait for the three months to be up. I had to tell her I wanted this to work, that I wanted to be there for her and the kids. But it was too late. By the time I got there, the apartment was empty. I called her and called her. Finally, she showed up with a couple of police officers. They told me that I needed to leave the apartment immediately. I asked if I could hug my kids, and they said yes, but I couldn't go back into the apartment or take anything with me. I hugged my kids. They were crying, so I started to cry.

Then they said I had to go. I walked to my car with just the clothes on my back. Eight years of hard work, and I was leaving with nothing. My kids were too young to know how much it hurt me to leave them. All these goals I had made to be the greatest dad, and I never even got to buy the jersey.

It would take far too long to go into the details of everything that happened after that. Apparently my wife had heard about the "Violence Against Women Act" (VAWA). This law made it so if a woman could prove she was a domestic abuse victim, she could become legal in the United States. I was arrested several times on charges that she completely made up. My kids were told lies. I was given a restraining order. After one particular criminal court, the State Prosecuting Attorney found me in the hall. She told me that she had now worked on six of the cases my wife had put against me. She said, "Obviously I have to tell you this off the record, as I shouldn't be giving you legal advice, but if I were you, I would run as far as you possibly can. Get away from her. Get where she can't put a case against you."

So that's what I did. I got in my car and just started driving, hoping the whole time that one day, my kids would understand. That one day, they would know that I hadn't wanted to leave them.

Fast forward to now, nine years later. I'm remarried, I have two more kids. I buy them treats. They run to me when I come home every day. I have a house with a yard and a dog. I have a job that I enjoy and provides well for our family. I have a wife who loves me. Yes, we fight. We have problems. But we apologize to each other and we fix it. I had no idea that life could be so happy. I had no idea that I could be so happy.

I grew up my whole life hearing stories about women in abusive relationships. I was in Mexico; women get abused there all of the time. You rarely hear about men being abused. As I look back at my first marriage, I realize that's what it was. I was in an abusive relationship. I was a man in an abusive relationship, and I didn't even know it.

I'm so glad that I was able to escape it, to get out, and to move forward. If I could have known the happiness that lay ahead of me, I would have escaped much sooner. Life is so different in a healthy relationship. You make decisions together. You work together. You play together. Yes, you make mistakes, but you learn to forgive. You learn to communicate, to work at it, to grow together, to express your goals and figure out how to work on things together.

If I could give advice to my children, all of them, that would be the advice I would give them. Learn how to communicate, how to express yourself, and how to listen to others without judgement. Learn how to forgive. Learn to be honest with yourself and others. Learn what it means to have a healthy relationship. Having a happy life literally depends on you learning those things.

It may be too late for me to be there for my older kids. Maybe not. I honestly don't know. But I do know I'll have the opportunity to be there for my younger kids. I'll be there. Their mom will be there. We'll be at every game, recital, or whatever they're doing. I'll get to be the dad I've always wanted to be, because I'm in a relationship that allows me to do so. I'll finally get to buy the jersey.

Finding My Light

By Cecilia Segedy

---

ave you ever been in a really deep, deep slump with darkness surrounding you and no light in sight for a very long time? Then you wonder to yourself if you're ever going to be able to find your way out, fighting the demons in your head every day that tell you that you're not good enough, that there's no way that even God could or would love you, that you should just end your life, that the world would be better off without you. Well, let me tell you that this is all wrong. There is hope and you are worth more than what those demons in your head say you are. There's a reason you're here. You matter to those around you. Don't give up; keep on fighting the battle, one day at a time in baby steps.

This is where I was a few years ago: lowest of all lows, darkest of the dark with no light in sight. I was done with life and didn't believe that anyone could care about me or love me, even though I was surrounded by many people who loved and cared about me. Not even God could love or care about me. At least this is what I thought. I was a nobody; there was nothing special about me. Why would anyone love someone like me? Even though I hadn't done anything wrong, I was fighting the ugly nasty battle of depression and felt worthless and very unloved.

This is what the voice in my head kept telling me, until one day, a wonderful man named Gordon came into my life and showed me a different way. Gordon was just an ordinary man, and he loved to show people that he cared about them. He didn't just say he cared about people; he showed them. Gordon loved those around him for who they were, not what he wanted them to be. He sincerely loved you for you. He saw the best in each and every person around him. Gordon looked and saw people the way God would see them. He could tell that I was struggling and not happy with my life. He could see the true unhappiness and loneliness in my eyes. He wondered how he could help me see my true worth and what others saw in me.

I'm religious, and in my religion, we believe that God can give healing and comfort through a special prayer known in our church as a blessing. One of the ways that Gordon helped me see my true worth was by giving me a blessing that would change my life. Through this blessing, I came to learn how much the Lord truly loved me and that he had a plan and purpose for me on this earth. I learned how much the people around me cared about me and loved me. I started to see my self-worth and who I really was. My life changed for the better from that day on. I was able to see the light at the end of the dark tunnel that I was in. I was able to start seeing my self-worth and that I was important to those around me. I began to feel the love that others had for me. Because of this, I wanted to better my life and to become a better person for those around me.

I know, for a fact, if Gordon hadn't gone out of his way to help me realize this, I wouldn't be the person I am today. I would more than likely not even be here on this earth today. I wouldn't be able to help those around me who are struggling to see their true self-worth. I know now that God has a plan for me and that there are many reasons I'm on the earth still today. Even if you don't believe in God, each of us has a purpose on this earth, a reason we're meant to be here. Most of us find our purpose by doing things that make us genuinely happy. Gordon found his purpose in helping others feel noticed and loved. When things get tough, and I start having bad days, all I have to do is think about Gordon and the things he has taught me and I'm able to change those bad days into good. I'm able to find at least one positive thing to keep me going and put one foot in front of the other.

I later went on a volunteer service mission to Germany to teach others about God's love and the plan that God has for them. I wanted everyone around me to feel God's love and how much happiness it brings into a life without light. I never would have served a mission or even thought of serving a mission to bless other people's lives if Gordon hadn't helped me find my way back out of the deep dark depression stage that I was in.

While serving a mission in Germany, I was able to get the help that I needed to overcome some of the demons in my head that had been tearing me down since my childhood. I would have never gathered

73

the courage to get this help had I not had the sweet example that Gordon was.

From all of this I've been able to find my true self-worth and help those around me who are struggling to find theirs. Even though it hasn't been an easy road for me, in the end, it sure has been worth it. I've finally been able to trust those around me. I've been able to accomplish many things due to the inspiration and example that Gordon gave me.

One of the biggest accomplishments that I have been able to do because of Gordon was get married and become a mother and raise a family, something I never thought I'd be able to do because of the demons in my head that told me I'd never amount to much, that no guy would ever find me attractive.

I've been able to help many young people understand that they don't have to be embarrassed by their battles with depression. Depression is a real thing. Many have also come to understand that there are people out there who've been through those battles and are ready to help them fight back, so that they can see their true self-worth and become the person they've always wanted to become.

So, if you're ever doubting yourself and wonder if you're good enough, remember that you are good enough. You'll always be good enough. Even if you feel like you don't matter, don't give up. Keep going. The days *do* get better. Something simple that you can start doing today is look for one positive thing that happened during the day. It may be as simple as your favorite song playing on the radio, but hold onto that one positive thing. Then soon you'll be able to find two positive things. Little by little, you'll be able to see that although many bad things may happen during your day, there's always at least one positive thing. Pay attention to that one thing. Give it light and help it find roots. If you don't know how, then ask for help. There's someone in your world who has been through what you're going through, and they're waiting to help you pull through too. You are worth it. You are loved.

Choosing My Career Path

By Rachelle Holbrook

$\mathcal{T}$he number of years ago that this story occurred was longer than I want to admit; however, I remember it like yesterday, and I've reflected on it many times…

I was a college student in my second year and nearly ready to receive my associate degree. The problem was that I had no idea what I wanted to choose as a career path. Where I attended school next depended upon my focus of study. It's difficult to know which Universities and programs to apply to when you haven't decided what you want your career to be. As a student who was paying her own way through college, knowing what to pursue was important for many reasons, the most important of which was to avoid paying for education in a career that I wouldn't find satisfying. I already wondered how many classes I had paid for that weren't going to contribute to whatever I ended up doing.

My real love at the time was music. But a career in music? I wasn't sure I wanted that. I knew I didn't have what it would take to teach music in a school setting, and I didn't feel competitive enough to want to try to make a public career in music. As the daughter of two teachers, it seemed everyone suggested that I choose teaching as a career. However, I had seen the long hours put in before and after school hours, administrations that wanted more from teachers while parents and students were mostly unappreciative and often critical. It seemed from my parents' examples that I knew more about what I *didn't* want than what I did want to do. The problem was, how could I find out what I DID want?

The possibilities seemed overwhelmingly endless. Out of desperation and grasping at what felt like a slim chance, I decided to schedule an appointment with my clergy to see if he could help me with the situation.

I think I went with the expectation that he would profoundly tell me some inspired career choice that God had whispered in his ear. I entered his office expecting that when I left, I would know what career I should pursue. I vaguely remember explaining to him the situation and how desperately I needed an immediate answer. I probably mentioned admission times were fast drawing to a close, and, truth be told, I hoped for scholarships and needed to figure out where I was going so that I might apply for scholarships. It seemed my life was at a standstill until I could figure a career choice out! It didn't take long to have my struggles and frustrations tumble out. As I finished my explanation, I remember thinking something like, Okay, now you know the problem; give me the solution!

Instead, I remember he just looked at me. He looked at me long enough for my heart to sink, long enough that I knew he wasn't going to give me a career answer choice. It felt like an uncomfortably long space of silence. Instead of direction for a career choice I hoped for, he said, "Do something that comes easy to you."

"What?" I asked, sure that this answer wasn't going to be helpful at all.

"Do something that comes easy to you," he repeated. Then he expounded. "A career that comes easy to you will be a joy. You don't want to have a career that's difficult because then you dread going to work every day. You want to wake up excited to go to work because it's easy for you and a job that you love. And if you do something that comes easily to you, then you don't have to spend extra time gathering skills that don't seem to come naturally, and then later deciding that career isn't for you. It will be a satisfying career if it's something you're naturally good at and comes easily to you. And if what you originally go into comes easy, your mind will work in such a way in that career that you'll be able to build upon that skill and grow and expand your abilities to further your career. Then promotions will come. God will be able to use your skills to bless others. Choose a career that comes easily to you," he reiterated.

"Oh," he said as if he'd just had an idea, "You could also go to {this person} and tell them you would like to take the test he created to help students figure out career choices."

I thanked the clergy for his time, contacted the person he suggested, and took the test.

Within a couple of days, I had made a career choice and was able to make the decisions I needed to pursue my education. To be clear, "Choose something that comes easy to you" does not mean that I chose to be lazy in my career choice. It meant I chose a career where the knowledge and skills were ones that came easily. This advice has helped me better balance a career and family and has given me the time and opportunities to help others better their lives.

I've reflected on this advice multiple times in my life when promotions have come or I've been given other opportunities for change or advancement. My clergy probably could have suggested careers for me, but he gave me something more precious: Advice that has enhanced my life while bringing happiness. It's wise advice that can be used for all. I'm so grateful he shared it with me: Do something that comes easy to you.

Unity

By Esther Paul

———

Sometimes, we experience moments in life when we know things will never be the same again. We were a young family, juggling crazy work schedules where the only time we were all together was a precious 15 minutes for dinner between the time I got home from work and my husband went to one of two part-time jobs. This was never in the plans. I had graduated with my bachelor's degree before we got married and he graduated just over a year later. We would have a year and a half for him to find his first full-time position and save up some money before adding a baby to the mix. Fast forward and our baby was over a year old and that full-time position had yet to happen. I wasn't sure the opportunity to be a stay-at-home mother would ever be mine.

After living with the crazy schedule for months on end, things were starting to fall into place. We both had full-time employment and could be home together in the evenings! In just three months, benefits would kick in and I would be able to transition to being at home. I was finally going to live my life-long dream of being with my baby. Those first two months were sweet. Spending my time with the people I loved. We were living the "picture perfect" life of a young family trying to make their way in the world and all their dreams were about to come true.

That all came crashing down when my husband and I sat down to talk about life one Friday night. What I expected to be a conversation about working through our little differences and quirks, turned into a conversation that would send me on a free fall of questioning everything I had known and trusted. The words "sex addiction" and "since high school" hit my ears and ricocheted through my whole body. I remember thinking, *Is our marriage over? How do I process this information? Was there any truth to the past five years?* Imagine taking everything you know about life and adding a question mark to all of it... I was in a perpetual cloud of collapse.

The first time I attended a support group for family and friends of addicts; I was frozen, poised, shattered, hesitant, anxious, wary, broken, and floundering. This should never have been part of my life experience. Coming to this group for some requirement in a university class, sure! But coming because of an intimate relationship with an addict, never. This was beyond anything I had imagined.

The facilitators opened the meeting, we read from a book of support principles, and the meeting was opened for sharing. One person volunteered to go first, and the sharing continued around the circle one by one with an occasional pass. Each share was familiar. Each share was personal. Each share had bits of my story (even the bits I had yet to learn). With each share, the room was full of empathy and space to sit in the others' pain with a prayer for healing.

My turn. It was now my turn to share. Do I hold myself in a bit more and just long enough to say, "pass," or do I risk my shattered pieces being scattered throughout the room with little to no hope of recovery? I draw a deep breath.

"I'm Esther."

The others say, "Hi Esther" in response.

Another deep breath.

"This is my first time… Two weeks ago…"

A few short sentences of my story make it past my lips as streams of tears and pain leave my body for the first time since "D-day." I was feeling. This was really my life. The bad dream that I wished would end really was my life. The next thing I know, the meeting is over and group members are expressing their love and inviting me to come again next week.

The next week seemed like a lifetime as my husband and I kept trying to navigate uncharted territory. I needed an outlet. I needed the relief that comes from being vulnerable with understanding hearts. So, I went back to the group. There, it was a relief to be with others who understood and were willing to help carry my burden. Each week, the women in the group helped me see things more clearly, and, slowly, my pain was easier to carry and easier to let go. Surrounded by women of all ages and backgrounds, I felt strong. The details of our stories were different, but the pain was always familiar. There began to be an army of support to help me navigate the unknown, let go of the old pain, and share the new pains. Through this healing, I could start to sit with the other women in their pain. We were living despite our circumstances. Like the ebb and flow of the tide, we adjusted and adapted to the needs of each member of the group.

How could such a strength come from a group of women experiencing deep trauma? I had never experienced anything like it. Differences were set aside, and we united in our quest for healing. We created a safe place. It was a time and space for understanding, loving, embracing, healing, and clarity. These strangers became some of my closest friends. We share a part of life that left each of us in isolation, gasping for breath, and no one to turn to for help. We got to know each other from the inside out, rather than the outside in. They helped me find hope and healing when I wasn't sure if there were any to be found. In sharing our pain, we've found our joy.

While I never wish pain or sorrow on anyone, I sincerely wish everyone could feel the unity and compassion from such a strong group of women. It's sacred. When looking at other people, you're tempted to think, *They have a perfect life* or *They could never understand.* Those are lies to keep us in isolation and sorrow. Heartache that threatens to take our life and soul away has been, is being, or will be experienced by each of us. A healing greater than ourselves will take over when we join together. The miracle is that healing comes even when we're all gasping for air.

Do I still feel pain? Yes. Does the memory still hurt? Yes. Are there still things we have to work through every day? Yes. But now I'm slower to judge, quicker to seek understanding, and sincerely want the best for others.

For those in isolation, please reach out. Others are feeling just as you do. But you must take the first step and reach out to find them. Help and hope will be there. I had no idea how many support groups are out there until I searched for one and found mine with complete strangers who understood exactly what I'm going through and who have now become my friends.

People are so good at hiding their pain. It feels easier to stay in isolation so that no one has to know what you're going through. The universal truth, however, is that life is hard, and we're unified through our trials. Everyone has them. Today is the day to ask for help in getting through your trial, whatever it may be.

Being a Light, Even in Your Darkest Days

By Brooke Vaquerano

----

can't remember my first interaction with Evelyn, but what I do know is that every interaction I had with her was positive and happy. I grew up in a neighborhood full of children. Their mothers were like my own. Evelyn's children were all older than me, but that didn't matter. I could knock on Evelyn's door anytime I wanted and she would invite me in and have a treat for me. "Brookie Cookie!" she'd say with a smile that lit up her whole face. "Come in!" We'd go straight to the kitchen where she would open the freezer and get me an orange dream bar or to the cookie jar and get me a cookie. Sometimes, I would even sit at the table and talk with her. She'd talk to me like I was her best friend, but I know I wasn't the only one who felt that way. It was well known that Evelyn was everyone's friend no matter their age. She never said she had more important things to do, although as a mom myself now, I know she had plenty to do.

When Evelyn was only 39 years old, she was diagnosed with Multiple Sclerosis. If it weren't for her physical limitations, you would have never known she struggled. She kept a smile on her face and kept laughing. She kept listening to everyone else and stayed upbeat. She kept up traditions like holding Easter egg hunts for everyone in the neighborhood. It was as if her life mission were to make everyone who came into contact with her forget all their problems and find a way to be happy.

Evelyn lived the next 21 years of her life full of love and happiness. She continued to lose mobility, ending up in a wheelchair. She and her husband moved to a neighboring city where she would be able to get around in her wheelchair better. She would always come back to the neighborhood to visit, having her family drive her around to visit people and bring them gifts. Anytime I would go to visit Evelyn, she wouldn't let me leave without taking something with me.

She eventually was no longer able to take care of herself or be cared for by her family. She spent the last 5 years of her life in a care center where her goal was still to make others happy. She would go around to others who weren't feeling well or who were sad, bring them little gifts, and cheer them up. She didn't worry about herself and her own hardships. She even stayed positive over the last year of her life being in a care center during the COVID-19 pandemic where she was only able to visit friends and family over the phone or through her outside window.

In April 2021, Evelyn was diagnosed with cancer and given a couple of months to live. She celebrated her 60th birthday in May and in June 2021, she passed away. Even while she was sick, she still would give her loved ones smiles and be happy to see them. She was a light for others her entire life.

I love Evelyn and I'm so grateful she was part of my village. She taught me to love others without conditions, to treat children with kindness and respect, to serve others no matter what you're going through, and that there's always a reason to be happy. I know she continues to bless lives up in heaven and even our lives here on Earth. I've been blessed to know my dear friend, Evelyn Parry.

In the Neighborhood

As told by Ryan Davis

There are three examples that come to mind almost immediately when asked who inspired me as a youth. Well, four really. But one of them is Jack Thomas, whose story is in this book. So I'll focus on the other three.

Growing up, I lived in a small town. Almost everyone knew everyone else. There were town gatherings and town work projects where we got to know each other, and, honestly, I was surrounded by a lot of really good people. I could choose almost any of them from my youth to talk about. Here, however, I'm just going to put three stories that all tie in to who I am today.

When I was young, my dad had a small farm where we raised a variety of animals. We had a mother pig ready to give birth. She started to have some complications as she was about to deliver her litter. She seemed to be struggling more than usual, and my dad became very concerned that he was going to lose her and her new litter of pigs. He called one of our neighbors, Andy

Larsen, who specialized in pig farming. Andy was in another town and knew he couldn't get there fast enough, so he told my dad to call his son Mark.

Mark arrived just in time to help the sow with the birth. He reached into the mother and could feel that one of the piglets was breeched inside and wasn't allowing any of the piglets to come out. Mark turned the piglet, and almost immediately, the sow started delivering her piglets one after another. If I remember correctly, it was a pretty big litter, maybe around 9 piglets, all of which would have been lost, and the mother herself, had Mark not shown up just when he did.

My dad and Mark were watching the piglets and making sure they were nursing correctly. With their attention on the pigs, they didn't notice Mark's father Andy drive up. He'd come straight from where he had been to make sure everything was all right. As he walked up behind my dad and his son Mark, he heard my dad say, "Well, thank you, Mark. How much do I owe you?"

Mark laughed and said, "Well gee, I don't know. Maybe twenty bucks?"

My father was about ready to pull out his wallet when Andy walked up behind Mark and whacked him on the back of the head. He calmly said, "I thought I taught you better than that!" Then he whacked my dad on the back of the head and said, "And I KNOW you were taught better than that!" Then he said something I'll never forget. He said, "This town is so great because we were taught to help each other without expecting anything in return. You help each other just to help each other. That's how we make it through because we're there to help each other. If you start expecting things from each other, you'll ruin it. Just help people because that's the right thing to do, not because you think you're going to get anything back in return." Then he asked about the pigs, and the discussion turned from there.

My dad rarely talks about that story. I honestly think he was embarrassed by getting his behavior corrected as a grown adult with kids. Mark was also an adult by then. I think that's what struck me about it, though: two grown men being scolded by their elder and being told that what mattered most was to help each other.

Following along that train of thought, during my first semester at college, I maintained a job that was close to my hometown. I would live on campus at the college during the school week, but on the weekends, I would come home and work in the fruit orchards near my home.

At this time, I was feeling quite a bit of pressure from my family and community to go on a two-year service mission. It was common in my church and community for young men to graduate high school and then go on a service mission for two years. However, I just didn't feel ready. I didn't think I knew enough or was good enough and I didn't feel like I was ready to commit that much time and effort into something I felt completely inadequate about.

One Saturday night, when I was working late at the orchard, my boss, whom I sincerely respected and looked up to, asked me to carry out some boxes of apples that an older gentleman had just purchased. There were a lot of boxes. I think almost 10 that I helped this gentleman carry out to his car. The man was very grateful and tried to give me a tip. I told him no, that was fine. I was glad to help him. He didn't need to pay me (I remembered the lesson from Andy Larsen). Just as he was trying to pay me, my boss walked out. The gentleman said, "Oh, I get it. It's late on a Saturday night. This must be your son, and that's why he won't take a tip."

My boss, Chad Rowley, smiled and said, "Actually he's not my son. But he's a darn good kid, and if I ever have a son, I want him to grow up to be just like Ryan."

My heart swelled with pride as I heard those words. Here was someone whom I really respected saying he hoped his future son turned out like me. I realized that I must be doing better than I thought I was doing, and I suddenly knew I needed to go on that service mission I had been putting off. I knew Chad well enough to know that he would want his son to go on a mission, and if he wanted his son to be like me, then I needed to go on a mission too. So I went. I ended up learning the Spanish language and other skills that have served me my entire life. I'm forever grateful for Chad and his kind words about me.

My other example of kindness and service was a man I always called Uncle Ken growing up. I think I was almost a teenager before I realized that he wasn't really my Uncle. I don't even know if we were related. Maybe he was distantly. But my whole life growing up, I called Ken Thomas my Uncle Ken.

Uncle Ken was always around helping people in our neighborhood. He would mysteriously appear whenever you were in the middle of a work project. And whenever you asked him why he was there, he would say, "Well, I was in the neighborhood and saw that you might need help, so I thought I'd stop by." Growing up, I always thought that we were just lucky that he happened to be in the neighborhood and saw us working.

As an adult, however, I learned the truth. On accident really. Uncle Ken was an electrician by trade. I was newly married and was trying to remodel a house that my wife and I had purchased about an hour away from my hometown. I called Uncle Ken because I had some electrical wiring questions. He explained how to run the wires and then asked when I was going to be working on this project. I told him I was out of town, but I would probably work on it in about two days.

Two days later, as I was working on my remodel, Uncle Ken showed up. I asked him what he was doing there and he said, "Well, my daughter and some grandkids live up here, so I was in the neighborhood. Thought I'd stop by and see if you needed any help." He then proceeded to rewire my entire remodel. I think he was there for over two hours connecting all of the wires to the electrical box. He pretty much did the entire thing for me. Then he told me thank you, that that was a good practice run since the next weekend he would be rewiring the electricity at a Girls' Camp facility.

I thanked him profusely, as I knew that Uncle Ken would never take anything (he was also raised by the same principles as Mr. Larsen), and wished him luck on his Girls' Camp project.

Later, I learned from one of the managers at the Girls' Camp that Uncle Ken had just shown up there and spent the whole day rewiring the camp for free. When the manager asked who had sent him, he just smiled and said, "Oh, I was just in the neighborhood and heard you needed help." The Girl's Camp is almost two hours from where Uncle Ken lived, and it was in the middle of nowhere. There's no way Uncle Ken was just "in the neighborhood." It was then that I realized what had been happening my whole youth. Uncle Ken would hear that someone needed help and he would make a point to be "in the neighborhood." I've thought of his example often when I have heard of my own family, friends, or neighbors in need of help. I've done my best to follow Uncle Ken's example and be "in the neighborhood" when help is needed.

I'm so grateful for these good men in my life. They've shaped the man I am today. And the amazing part is that there are so many more examples of good men who influenced me that I don't have space to include them in this short story. I truly was blessed with amazing examples of goodness and kindness growing up. I had good examples of women as well, but the examples that stuck out to me most were the men because, as a youth, I was trying to figure out what kind of man I wanted to be, so I was watching the men in my life pretty closely. I'm grateful for good men, great men really, who showed me by example how to be a good man myself. I hope that I can pay it forward, as they did, and help influence the young men of the next generation to grow up to be good men, serving others without expecting anything in return.

Leaders Are Readers

By Rosilee Barreto

When I was in college, just weeks after reading my first self-help book, I went to a leadership seminar on campus where we were to hear a speech from James LeVoy Sorenson. I didn't even know who he was; I just knew that he was going to be talking on a subject similar to one in the book I had read, so I was interested in learning more.

Within five minutes of his speech, I found out that he was a billionaire. He had invented many different groundbreaking medical devices and equipment for his time, including the disposable facemask, something highly used to this day.

I don't remember a lot of what he said that day; I was honestly in awe of the idea that I was in the same room as a billionaire. But I do remember a phrase that he used somewhere in the middle. He read a quote that I've sinced learned is attributed to Harry S. Truman, "Not all readers are leaders, but all leaders are readers." Mr. Sorenson then went on to say that our own personal development is the most critical habit we could possible develop in this life. He said, "The only person that can possibly improve your life is you. Don't wait for 'your ship to come in.' Go out and build a ship."

I've never forgotten that. From somewhere deep inside of me, I suddenly had a desire to "build a ship" or in other words, create something that would lead to financial success.

I started to read books by successful entrepreneurs. I started to listen to speeches and watch videos. I even tried to start my own business twice. I failed both times.

I had so much desire in me to succeed, but all I ended up doing was failing. Or, at least, so I thought.

Ten years after I heard that speech by James LeVoy Sorenson, I was living in a little room on the second story of a barn. Yes, a barn. The barn was built in the early 1900s when stable boys lived above the horses or in the carriage house. My husband and I had just gotten married. Because of bad financial decisions on both of our parts, and some hefty attorney fees remaining from my husband's previous marriage, we started our marriage together with substantial debt. Hence, the barn. We lived in the little room and cleaned the horse stalls every morning as rent.

The room was so small that all we could fit inside it was a twin bed and one dresser. There was no bathroom. To use the bathroom, we had to go down the barn stairs, across the yard, and into the main house. About three weeks into our marriage, I got a pretty bad bladder infection. I woke up one morning and had to pee SO bad that I knew I would never make it to the main house. I grabbed the closest thing I could to relieve myself—a garbage can. As I was crouching, peeing in this garbage can, I suddenly became angry. Angry at myself. Angry at our situation. Angry that other newlyweds go on a cruises while I'm working two jobs, cleaning horse stalls, and peeing in a garbage can.

I made my mind up right then that we were going to fix things. I had a heart-to-heart with my husband when he got home from his second job. I told him we were going to read one finance book a month until we got out of the mess we were in.

We actually realized very quickly that it would be easier for us to listen to audiobooks, as we both had jobs where headphones were allowed. We also both had to commute to our jobs. So during our commute, and during each shift of each job, we committed to listening to one chapter, which was about three chapters a day. Sometimes, we got more in, and sometimes less, but we listened to as much as could, then had a discussion at the end of the day about what we learned.

We first read *Rich Dad, Poor Dad* by Robert Kiyosaki. Then we read *The Richest Man in Babylon* by George Clason, which we listened to twice in a row. The third book we both really enjoyed and listened to several times in a row: *The 10 Secrets of Abundant Wealth* by Adam J. Jackson. After that, we kind of separated ways so we could fit more books in. He would listen to a book and tell me what he learned from it, and I would do the same. He read *The Alchemist* by Paulo Coehlo and I read *Secrets of the Millionaire Mind* by T. Harv Eker. He listened to *My Philosophy for Successful Living* by Jim Rohn and I listened to *The Total Money Makeover* by Dave Ramsey.

We continued this way, book after book. Our goal was to take one thing from each book and apply it to our financial situation. We have now read way too many books to list here, but each one has been beneficial, and has offered an idea that came right when we needed it.

After six months, we were able to get an apartment (with a bathroom in our bedroom!). We were both still working two full-time jobs, but we were able to use our first jobs to pay the bills and the second jobs to pay off debt and build a savings account. After two years and more than $50,000 of debt paid, we were able to start a business that was successful. After three years, we had all of our debt paid off, over $80,000, and were able to move into a 4-bedroom, 2-bath rental house. My husband was now running the business full-time, and I was helping him run the back office side and bookkeeping while maintaining one of my full-time jobs.

We decided then, with our debt paid off, that it was time to start a family together. We started saving up for the baby and continued saving throughout my pregnancy. Unfortunately, our son's birth was actually double the amount of money we had saved up for the birth, so we did backtrack a little and go back into debt. However, we pulled out of it quickly and were able to buy a house a year later. I was also able to quit my last full-time job and be home full-time with our son.

After a year of living happily in our new home, we added a second child to the mix. We had just expanded a section of our business and believed we would really be on our way. However, six months later, our business fell apart. We had tried to expand too far too soon, with not enough qualified employees, and it all fell out from underneath us. My husband decided to go to a trade school and expand his career during the day while I found a job and worked nights to pay the bills.

Gratefully, we didn't forget the skills we had learned from our initial financial rut. Within one year, we had another business up and rolling, this one with NO employees. I was able to quit my night job, and we went back to my husband running the front end of the business while I stayed home with the kids and ran the back office and paperwork of the business.

By this time, my husband's older kids (from his previous marriage) were living with us. Since they were all teenagers, life got a little crazy. They had school activities going on, homework they needed help with, and there was never a dull moment. During their time with us, I bought the *Foundations in Personal Finance: Middle School Edition for Self-Study* from the Dave Ramsey website and began working through it with them. I shared with them their father's and my finance journey and explained that I never wanted them to have to experience what we went through.

When one of my friends found out I was teaching finance to my kids, she asked if I could come give a short talk about finance to a youth group she supervised. I made a one-page printout of the biggest points of finance that I wished I would have known as a teenager and young adult. I was nervous on my way to give the talk and, in fact, at the beginning of my speech as well, but as I kept talking and sharing my story, I realized I was actually enjoying myself . I had no idea how much I enjoyed public speaking, especially to teenagers! I wasn't sure if any of my message would get through to the kids, but afterwards, one of the youth who had been there sent me a message and asked if she could get the digital copy of the print-out. She said she had learned a lot and wanted to discuss the printout with her family.

I can't even describe the amount of satisfaction and happiness I felt after she sent that message. I suddenly realized that I wanted to speak again. I decided to enroll in an online course about building an online business and becoming a public speaker, and have continued to move forward in that direction.

Even though my progress has been slow, and at the time of writing this book, I've yet to accomplish all of my goals, I often think about the advice given by Mr. Sorenson at his seminar, that the most critical habit we could possibly cultivate is our own personal development.

I often wonder where my husband and I would be now if we hadn't taken the initiative to work on ourselves and our finances. We would probably still be working two or three jobs each, never seeing each other, and wasting our money on things that bring us more debt instead of freedom. If we would have still had kids in that situation, they would probably have been raised in daycare while we worked. I highly doubt we would ever have been able to purchase a home or have as much quality time together as we're able to enjoy at this time.

I remember thinking when I got out of high school that I was FINALLY done with school and could just work or have fun. I've since realized that our education never stops. We have the option to learn new things every day. Those who make an effort to learn as much as they can through personal study, work, or educational opportunities are that much more prepared for whatever opportunities cross their paths or the opportunities that they create for themselves.

My advice to anyone who feels like they're stuck in a rut in life or that something is missing is to figure out what you really want. If you take the time to figure out what you really want in life, then you can start advancing toward it. You can look around and find someone who's really good at what you're lacking and start learning how to do what they do.

For instance, back when we were living in that small room in a barn, my husband and I figured out what we were severely lacking most at the time was understanding our finances. Our lack of knowledge of how to manage our finances, conquer bad spending habits, and learn what to save for and invest in was severely affecting our quality of life. We had to make a decision together to learn all we could about these three areas of finance in order to better our quality of life significantly.

Now that we have our finances under control, we've moved on to other things we feel that we're lacking and would like to progess in. For my husband, it's learning how to communicate and express himself effectively. For me, it's learning time management and how to be a more patient and loving wife and mother. We are both learning things that are unique to us and what we're lacking, but we're helping each other in our desire to progess. We have a stronger marriage and are more effective working together because we sincerely strive to improve ourselves and work toward our goals.

Everyone is in a different situation, and there are many things in this life that you cannot control. You can't control your friends' actions, you can't control your partner, you can't control your kids, you can't control the weather, you can't control your car breaking down in the middle of rush hour traffic, etc. The list could go on and on of things that are outside your control. However, you CAN control your education. You CAN control your personal growth and development. You CAN control how much you learn and what the subjects are. You CAN control your goals and the direction your life is moving in. Take the time to figure out what would sincerely make you happier, and then work to improve in that area by study, apprenticeship, work, or classes. Find a way to work toward what you want most in life, and don't give up! You're always closer than you think to achieve something that you may have never thought possible.

Thank you for reading!

If you've enjoyed this book, please leave a five star review on Amazon using the following link: *https://www.amazon.com/dp/B09HSMQ2PF*

Be Inspirational

A second book of *Productive Toilet Time* is already in production. If you would like share your short story about an inspirational person or event in your life, please contact the author through email at info@rosileebarreto.com, through the contact form on her website at www.rosileebarreto.com, or on Facebook at https://www.facebook.com/RosileeBarreto.

DOWNLOAD YOUR FREE GIFT!

Want to listen to Productive Toilet Time on the go?

Grab your free audiobook here:
https://rosileebarreto.com/free-audiobook-download/

About the Author

Rosilee Barreto enjoys most her roles as a wife and mother. When she's not writing, she enjoys spending quality time with family, riding horses, running, reading, exploring nature, and teaching personal finance to beginners. You can find out more about Rosilee and her future books at www.rosileebarreto.com. You can also follow her on Facebook, Instagram, and Amazon.

Made in the USA
Las Vegas, NV
10 November 2021

34139797R00066